Critical Thinking for
Sports Students

Active Learning in Sport – titles in the series

To order, please contact our distributor: BEBC Distribution, Albion Close, Parkstone, Poole, BH12 3LL. Telephone: 0845 230 9000, email: **learningmatters@bebc.co.uk**. You can find more information on each of these titles and our other learning resources at **www.learningmatters.co.uk**.

Critical Thinking for Sports Students

Emily Ryall

LearningMatters

First published in 2010 by Learning Matters Ltd

British Library Cataloguing in Publication Data
A CIP record for this book is available from the British Library.
ISBN 978 1 84445 457 0
This book is also available in the following ebook formats:
Adobe ebook   ISBN: 978 1 84445 679 6
EPUB ebook   ISBN: 978 1 84445 678 9
Kindle   ISBN: 978 1 84445 980 3

Cover and text design by Toucan Design
Project management by Swales & Willis Ltd, Exeter, Devon
Typeset by Kelly Winter
Printed and bound in Great Britain by TJ International Ltd, Padstow, Cornwall
Learning Matters Ltd
33 Southernhay East
Exeter EX1 1NX
Tel: 01392 215560
info@learningmatters.co.uk
www.learningmatters.co.uk

FSC
Mixed Sources
Product group from well-managed
forests and other controlled sources
Cert no. SGS-COC-2482
www.fsc.org
© 1996 Forest Stewardship Council

To my family

Contents

Preface and acknowledgements

I was fortunate enough as an undergraduate to be taught critical thinking by some very eminent scholars in the field, most notably Anne Thomson and Alex Fisher. However, whilst critical thinking is a fundamental requirement for succeeding at university level, too few students are explicitly taught to develop the necessary skills. In the absence of dedicated modules in critical thinking this textbook is an attempt to provide a resource that can be used in the field of sports studies and sports sciences. It attempts to appeal specifically to students studying sport by illustrating how critical thinking skills are necessary for their studies and their lives in the world beyond academia. It is designed purely as an introduction and overview of the subject and not to be considered as anywhere near a definitive guide. In fact, in my research for this book, I have come to accept that the subject of critical thinking is too broad to be captured in any single text (although Ennis's (1996) book comes close). There are aspects of critical thinking that I would have liked to have included but haven't been able to and others that are only mentioned very briefly. As such I hope readers will use the further reading sections to point them to texts that provide a much deeper analysis and explanation of many of the issues. Bearing this in mind, any criticisms or suggestions for improvement would still be welcomed.

The article by Yasmin Alibhai-Brown in Chapter 7 is reprinted by permission of Telegraph Media Group Limited; the article by Ed Smith in Chapter 7 is reprinted by permission of Independent News and Media.

I would like to thank those at Learning Matters; in particular Anthony Haynes for approaching me and getting me started, and Helen Fairlie for her editorial work.

Emily Ryall
April 2010

Chapter 1
Critical thinking and the study of sport

Learning Objectives

This chapter will help you:

- define the concept of critical thinking;
- recognise some of the skills that critical thinking requires;
- understand why the ability to think critically is a valuable attribute;
- identify the relationship between critical thinking and the study of sport.

Introduction

How would you respond to the following statement?

The study of sport doesn't require any great ability to think, does it? Surely it's just about running around on artificial turf all day?

Would you:

a) Look at the speaker blankly and walk away?
b) Quietly and nervously reply, 'yes, I suppose you're right'?
c) Respond aggressively by saying, 'you obviously don't know anything about it then!'?
d) Enter willingly into a discussion about the academic integrity of undergraduate courses in sport?

If you answered a, b, or c to the above then you might need some persuasion that critical thinking has an important role to play in your studies. If you answered d, you may already be aware of the importance of thinking critically and your skills in this area may be reasonably developed. Either way, the purpose behind this book is to demonstrate the value of critical thought and to help you hone and consolidate the skills it requires.

What is critical thinking?

Essentially, the key to thinking critically is to: ask questions; decide what information is most accurate and relevant; establish what assumptions you are making; make reasonable and logical judgements; and be willing to subject all of your conclusions to yet more questioning (Figure 1.1).

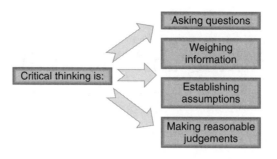

Figure 1.1.

Learning Activity 1.1

Decide whether you already believe the following statements to be true or whether you would need further information before you could decide. Are they all the same types of statement? Provide a justification for your answer.

a) The Ukrainian Oleksandr Petriv broke the 25m rapid fire pistol shooting record in the Beijing 2008 Olympics.
b) Water polo is a sport.
c) Hitler attempted to use the 1936 Berlin Olympics as a vehicle to promote his Nazi ideology.
d) In 100 years time, Formula One racing will no longer exist.
e) Muscles require adenosine triphosphate to function.
f) Boxing should be taught as part of the PE curriculum in every secondary school.

Why is it so important to think critically?

The ability to think independently and critically is a key facet of higher education regardless of the subject you are studying. Developing the ability to think critically allows better informed and justified decisions to be made. Being able to provide clear and reasonable justification for the decisions you make and the action you subsequently take will provide you with credibility, influence, respect and, ultimately, the power to make more decisions and hold greater responsibility. Employers seeking graduates will often state essential criteria such as the ability to think critically, innovatively and independently. So improving your skills in this area will, at the very least, make you more employable. When employers advertise for applicants with a 'keen eye for detail', 'an ability to communicate ideas clearly' and 'a passionate interest in this area', they are essentially asking for the ability to think critically and to express ideas persuasively – key skills in almost any graduate-level job.

The ability to be critical is also part of what it means to be human. We are not creatures who react passively to our environment. We are able to reflect upon the way we live our life, the choices we make and the action we take as if detached observers. This unique ability is demonstrated in the use of imagery in sport and employed by sports psychologists to improve performance. The point of visualising an action as if a spectator and imagining the action performed effectively, i.e. a golf swing or kicking a ball, is to be able to reflect upon your movement and improve it. Furthermore, being able to imagine ourselves in various situations allows us to take all the knowledge and experience we have about the world and predict the future, or at least predict likely outcomes of particular courses of action. For instance, if I know that my opponent in my next tennis match likes to play from the baseline, then I can adjust my practice and game accordingly so as to take advantage of this. Ultimately, the best coaches are those who are able to think critically about the strengths and weaknesses of players and communicate this knowledge effectively.

So we could say that thought influences or directs behaviour. When we neglect to consider the consequences of our actions, we often later rue the fact that we didn't 'think'. In contrast, the ability we have to project our self into the future allows us to imagine the consequences of various courses of action and enables us to make informed decisions. When we act upon these decisions we are often expected to be able to justify and provide reasons for our actions. In this sense, thought is continuous with practice. One of the defining elements of higher education is to allow students to refine their critical thinking skills – to be willing and able to ask appropriate questions, to identify relevant and valid information, and to reach sound judgements.

Being able to think critically is also empowering. If we are able to think for ourselves then we are less subject to the control, whims and propaganda of others. The darker times in human history have been when people have acted without thinking critically about their beliefs, values and consequences. It is when people blindly follow others without questioning their arguments or motives that prejudice and suffering occurs. This is why it is not always easy to think critically (sometimes difficult and unpopular decisions need to be made) and why the moral virtues of courage and resolve are often required.

Critical thinking and moral courage

Sometimes the result of thinking critically leads to conclusions that may be difficult for us to act upon, especially if we have to defend ourselves in making unpopular decisions or make personal sacrifices. Sporting boycotts of politically sensitive events are a prime example of the times when individuals need to consider their own actions.

When Stuart MacGill, the Australian cricketer, decided not to make himself eligible for Australia's tour to Zimbabwe in 2004, he took the decision after careful and considered deliberation. MacGill reasoned that it would not be morally justifiable for him to participate in a cricket match that took place in a country that he believed was suffering under malevolent leadership. MacGill could have kept his head down and maintained, as many others had done, that sport and politics should be kept separate and that he was simply paid to play cricket and not to make political comments. In refusing to make himself eligible for selection, MacGill's place in the test side was forfeited, which could have had long-lasting effects on the rest of his career. Not only could MacGill have been accused of dissent against the cricketing authorities but also he would have to regain his selection for future tests. This was arguably an act of moral courage as, despite the consequences for himself, MacGill felt it necessary to take a publicised stand against the political situation in Zimbabwe. It was not a decision that MacGill took lightly; it was a decision reached after careful and considered thought, and one that he was confident in justifying to others.

Being able to think critically is a useful tool both to protect yourself against manipulation from others, to be a leader rather than a follower, and ultimately to have a role in creating the type of world in which you want to live. It is fundamentally necessary if we are to live up to our responsibilities as citizens in a human community.

Teach people to make good decisions and you equip them to improve their own futures and become contributing members of society, rather than burdens on society. Becoming educated and practicing good judgement does not absolutely guarantee a life of happiness, virtue, or economic success, but it surely offers a better chance at those things. And it is clearly better than enduring the consequences of making bad decisions and better than burdening friends, family, and all the rest of us with the unwanted and avoidable consequences of those poor choices.

(Facione, 2007, p1)

Learning Activity 1.2

a) Think of a time when you have had to make a difficult decision. What reasons made it difficult, what judgement did you make and how did you defend it?

b) Think of a time where you have been involved in a disagreement with someone else. Were you willing to argue your case, did you just enforce your position or did you end up blindly accepting the other's point of view? With the benefit of hindsight, would there be anything that you would have changed about your actions?

Isn't it just a matter of opinion?

On the way home from training, a team-mate comments, 'I can't believe Nicky wasn't selected for the game this weekend.' Another team-mate replies, 'No, it was definitely the right decision to select Becky instead.'

One common mistake that many students make is to think that every opinion is equally valid. If this was the case, then you would have nothing further to say about Karen's and Ally's disagreement. Yet if it is your responsibility for selecting the team, there will be times when you have to make difficult decisions with which not everyone will agree. How well you are able to make and justify these decisions is dependent on your ability to think critically. If you are in a position of responsibility whereby you are expected to make judgements and decisions (which is a key aspect of graduate-level employment) then it simply isn't possible to sit on the fence and maintain that it is just a matter of opinion.

I often see first-year undergraduates becoming exasperated with being constantly questioned about, and being asked to defend, their position on topics discussed in class. Occasionally, they exclaim in frustration, 'Just tell us the answer!' in the anticipation that I can supply them with the correct response. What all students will undoubtedly learn over the next few years if they are to succeed at undergraduate level is that even in the 'hard' sciences, i.e. physiology and biomechanics, nothing is definitive, and even the most uncontentious issues have opponents and alternative theories. Often the answer to a question is dependent on the reason that the question is asked. When you first start studying a subject it may be necessary to learn information as if absolute fact. It provides a foundation block on which to later develop and test more knowledge and theories. For instance, many first-year exam questions require specific answers that are considered by the academic and research community as being the 'best possible' at the time (*axiomatic statements*). There may also be mathematical, logical or definitional questions for which there is generally a specific answer that is self-contained within the concept (e.g. 'the square root of 16 is 4' or 'VO_2 max is a measurement of aerobic capacity') (*analytic statements*). These types of single 'correct' answers may be the ones that you have been most used to providing in your previous study.

Alternatively, it may be that the answers to some questions are purely dependent on personal preference or taste, for instance, the decision to take particular course options or the dissertation topic that you choose. Arguably, these are the questions that have little place in the academic world. For instance, whether one prefers the taste of one brand of sports energy drink over another is generally regarded as a matter of subjective opinion of which little can be said (unless one is interested in the reasons or causes underlying such preferences).

The type of question that you are most likely to be asked at undergraduate level is one that requires the skills of critical thought. Independent study or final year dissertations in particular are designed to require the student to show that they can reason logically and formulate original hypotheses. Even students that are being assessed on 'creative', 'aesthetic' or 'performance' elements in sport and dance will be required to provide a justification, interpretation and critique of their movements. Translating a particular dance as being representative of war or conflict requires thought as to why those two things are analogous – what is it about the movement of the performer that signifies a particular state of affairs in human life? Similarly, any attempt to discover the reasons as to why particular members of our society become involved in football hooliganism requires the assimilation of various pieces of evidence, connections to be made between possible explanations and hypotheses tested.

Case Study 1.1 focuses upon the question of whether performance-enhancing drugs should be allowed in sport. Two contrary positions are given, both providing justification for the position that they take. Richard Callicott, in the first, maintains that these drugs are both harmful and against the 'spirit of sport', whereas Carl Thomen responds with a counter-argument that we don't legislate on the basis of harm for other things in sport, such as racing motorcycles or boxing. Thomen also highlights examples in other areas of life where we are happy to seek perfection and improve performance. The discussion could (and does) go on but what it illustrates is that it is not just a matter of opinion but rather of reasoned judgement.

Case Study 1.1
Should performance-enhancing drugs (such as steroids) be banned in sports?

Yes:

Richard Callicott, former Chief Executive of UK Sport, stated:

> *As the national anti-doping agency we will never accept this. Performance-enhancing drugs are not only prohibited because they violate the spirit of sport but because they can damage the health of athletes. The idea of allowing them in sport could lead to a situation whereby sportsmen and women are used as human guinea pigs for a constant flow of new, unregulated substances. The long-term effects don't bear thinking about.*

No:

Carl Thomen, PhD candidate in Sports Philosophy at the University of Gloucestershire, wrote:

> *With reference to performance-enhancing drugs, if we have discarded the useless 'unfair advantage' argument because of an unbiased look at the inherently technologically unfair nature of professional sport, we are really only left with worries about harm to athletes. Please note: harm to athletes, not breast augmentation patients, Viagra users or the spaced-out Ritalin generation. We don't worry when the Isle of Man TT race or the Vendée Globe claims another life, or when that boxer on the news gets Alzheimer's. And when innocent Canadian soldiers are shot by American pilots buzzing on Army-sanctioned ephedrine, we're still convinced that sport is somehow exempt from the influence of the natural human desire for constant improvement.*

> *The rationalization is that it is okay for pilots to take performance-enhancing drugs, for musicians to use beta blockers and for our children to swallow Ritalin because performance is paramount. But where are our health concerns now? Perversely, we deny the 'performance is paramount' principle in professional sport while citing health concerns about performance-enhancing drugs. We want better performances from our sports heroes all the time, but demonize the methods used to produce such performances while hiding behind concerns for health that are not commensurate with our normal paternalistic attitudes.*

[Source: ProCon.org]

Types of statement

As illustrated by Learning Activity 1.1, critical thought requires the evaluation of different types of claim and evidence. Figure 1.2 indicates the three general types of answer that can be given depending on the question asked. Statements of fact are primarily dependent on agreed definitions or the results of reliable and verifiable scientific experiments. Statements of preference are personal and subjective likes and dislikes that aren't really open to rational discussion (e.g. there is not much one could say in response to someone who states a preference for banana-flavoured over chocolate-flavoured protein drinks). However, it is a statement of reason that marks a critical thinker out the most. Critical thinking requires an understanding of all three types of answers, though a good critical thinker is someone who is able to make and defend statements of judgement.

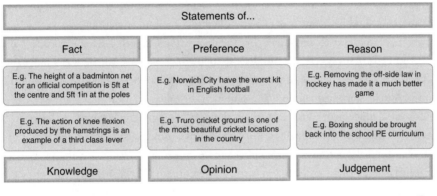

Figure 1.2.

Learning Activity 1.3

Decide whether the following statements are statements of fact, preference or reason, or a combination of these things. (For the purposes of this activity, don't worry too much about whether they are true or not.)

a) I don't enjoy having to train in the cold, wet and dark.
b) Games played on artificial turf are much faster than those played on grass.
c) The levels of financial investment required to compete in the Olympic Games means it is not a fair competition.
d) There is nothing more exciting than watching the Grand National directly from the stands.
e) Levels of obesity are rising in all developed, Westernised countries.
f) Sport is a valuable social tool to enhance the lives of disaffected young people.
g) The rectus abdominis, transversus abdominis, external oblique and internal oblique are the four muscles that make up the stomach muscles.
h) The England women's cricket team should have received the BBC Sports Personality 'Team of the Year' award in 2009.

Critical thinking and value judgement

The mark of a competent critical thinker is a person who is able to make judgements based on sound reasoning. It is not sufficient to merely sketch out various and competing positions; you must adjudicate between them. And once a judgement is made, action should follow. Difficult decisions often need to be made and justified and unfortunately most decisions in life do not come down to an undisputed set of facts. We often have to make value judgements, that is, we need to make decisions based on the things that we believe to be most important or valuable to human life. This is where the skills of critical thinking prove their worth. Generally, statements that provide a moral recommendation are value judgements whereas statements that offer descriptions of events are factual statements. For instance, when the British government decided to allocate more resources to funding the 2012 Olympics when it had gone over its initial budget, money was diverted that could have been spent elsewhere; on health, education or policing for example. A value judgement was made that money would be better spent on the Olympics than on something else.

However, it is important to remember that the distinction between a statement of fact and a statement of value isn't always clear. Consider the following example: 'Aurelie was a magnanimous winner.' That Aurelie was a winner is a statement of fact that can be verified by observation or records. That Aurelie was magnanimous is a statement of value.

Making a value judgement ultimately comes down to an individual's values, preferences, biases and prejudices. These can be rationalised through logical argument but more often than not they are indicative of emotional reactions that are either innate or acquired. Values are often very deep-seated and are hard to alter through rational argument. Differentiating between statements of fact and statements of value can be useful in our evaluation of arguments. If an argument is over whether high-board divers have shorter competitive careers than tennis players then there are means to discover an answer. However, if an argument simply comes down to personal preference, for instance, over whether high-board diving is more beautiful to watch than tennis, then there may be times when you simply have to agree to disagree.

Learning Activity 1.4

Decide which of the following statements are statements of fact and statements of value (or a mixture of both).

a) Wolves won 36–15 last weekend.
b) Richard will be selected to compete in Hong Kong.
c) The goalkeeper made a huge error by moving off his goal line.
d) You should rest if you want to recover quickly from your injury.
e) The league begins on 14 September.

f) You should go to training.

g) You should support Liverpool over Everton.

h) Ashley took the wrong route in the cross-country race.

i) Ethan was wrong to use steroids.

Making good judgements

The ability to make a good judgement requires a variety of skills and attributes. It requires the characteristics of honesty, openness and courage. As outlined in the example of Stuart MacGill pulling out of Australia's cricket tour of Zimbabwe, there may be times when the conclusions you reach are not ones that make you popular amongst your friends and peers, and may require you to make personal sacrifices. This is why it requires a mind that is open to making difficult decisions, and the virtues of courage and strength to act upon them. It also requires an honesty to acknowledge when you make mistakes in your reasoning and a willingness to listen to the reasoning of others. As will be shown throughout this book, critical thought is dependent on following arguments to their logical conclusion even if these conclusions may be disagreeable to some.

Good judgement requires the ability to weigh the significance of contrasting evidence. If this evidence relies upon the arguments and beliefs of others, questions need to be asked about the reliability of such statements. Does the person have an interest in persuading you to accept their argument? How credible are they in terms of their knowledge and experience in the field? Asking questions such as these enables you to interrogate arguments to a greater degree. It is to ask, what reason is there for believing or accepting a particular piece of evidence. Complete scepticism (the refusal to accept any evidence as sufficient justification) however, is neither possible nor desirable; there comes a point whereby evidence must be taken for granted (an axiom) and used as a foundation for other knowledge. What is considered 'truth' or 'reality' is dependent on the viewpoint that is being taken and the point in asking the question in the first place. As can be seen in optical illusions, the concept of 'objective reality' is much more complicated that might at first appear. However, for the purposes of critical thinking it is important to question the assumptions that you make in constructing arguments and reaching conclusions, even if you decide that they are assumptions that you simply have to accept as true for the sake of coming to any conclusion at all.

We also need to recognise our starting position and be open about our interests, prejudices and biases. For example, as a university-educated, middle-class British female from the south-west of England, I would be more likely to find and create examples that reflect my own interests (although I have tried to reflect a variety of sports and nationalities throughout), hence I will often use examples of female athletes and sports that I have played, and neglect to use examples of other cultures and ethnicities. If I were a native Alaskan writing this book, I would undoubtedly be more likely to use examples from my own heritage and culture. That is not to say that acknowledging one's individual identity, interests and personal preferences devalues the arguments or conclusions that I make, but it is important to openly lay these out in order to subject one's own thinking to critical reflection and to display to others that you are aware of the parameters by which, to a degree, you are constrained.

Essentially, the formation of good judgement is a positive enterprise that is constructive rather than destructive. Its aim is to direct action rather than merely to provide obstructive opposition, in order to engender the 'good life' or a life worth living (Figure 1.3).

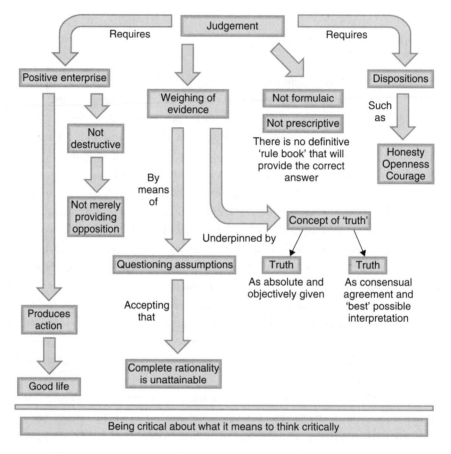

Figure 1.3.

Critical thinking as a game to be practised

Even if you're not particularly argumentative and don't naturally enjoy being involved in debates and discussion, the higher marks at degree-level study are achieved through demonstrating an ability to think critically about issues, and to argue and defend a position. The fact that you're reading this means at the very least you acknowledge that developing these skills is a game that must be played in order to succeed in higher education.

Thompson (2003, pp2–3) makes an analogy between developing critical thinking skills and improving the skills required for sport:

In common with other skills, reasoning skills can be improved and polished with practice. If we think of critical reasoning as analogous to a game, we can see it as involving a set of particular skills and also the ability to deploy this set of skills when engaged in planning the game. In tennis, for example, players need to be good at executing particular strokes – driving, volleying, serving. But, in order to win a game, they need to be able to put these skills together in an appropriate way, and also be able to respond to moves made by their opponent.

Although some people may find themselves at a natural advantage in thinking critically, just as some might show a natural predisposition to excel at racquet sports, it is possible for everyone to improve their ability through determination, patience and practice. Even for those who show a natural aptitude at arguing can improve their skills further; after all, who's ever heard of a player who just happened to win Wimbledon without practising their skills for years beforehand?

In summary, being a successful critical thinker begins with a particular outlook. This means trying to be as impartial and honest as possible and having the courage to follow arguments through to their logical conclusion (Figure 1.4).

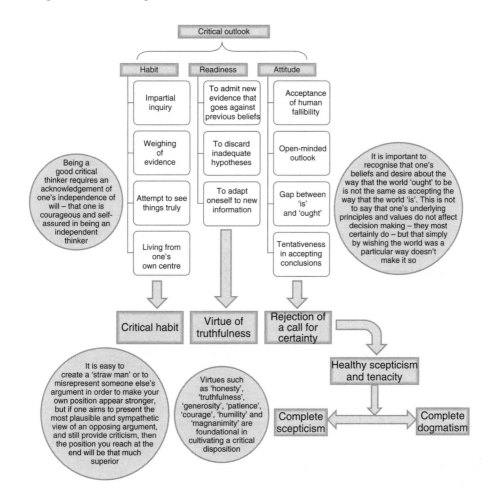

Figure 1.4.

Test Your Understanding

Learning Activity 1.5

State whether the following statements are true or false.

a) Critical thinking involves asking relevant questions and questioning assumptions.
b) There are some areas in the study of sport that don't require the ability to think critically.
c) Critical thinking is about reaching the correct answer.
d) The skills required in critical thinking are those required in graduate-level employment.
e) The ability to think critically requires the courage of openness, honesty and courage.
f) Statements of reason are those that can be defended and justified.
g) Value judgements are simply an expression of opinion.
h) The skills of critical thought can be easily acquired.

Chapter Review

What is critical thinking?

The ability to think rationally and reflectively, making sound judgements as to what action will best determine the desired outcome.

Why is critical thinking important?

There are many reasons but at the very least, it enables us as humans to reach our potential and direct our lives to how we wish to live. On a more pragmatic and immediate level, being able to think critically will enable you to reach the higher marks in degree-level study and encompasses many skills desired by graduate employers.

What attributes and skills does it require?

It requires the skill of asking questions, weighing information, questioning assumptions and reaching judgements. It also requires the courage to make difficult decisions and be open to new evidence and the persuasion of others.

What is a value judgement?

A value judgement is a decision made on an issue where there isn't a set of undisputed facts leading to a single conclusion. They are judgements about ethical or aesthetic issues and are based upon what you believe to be most important or valuable.

Further Reading

Blackburn, S (2001) *Think: A Compelling Introduction to Philosophy.* Oxford: Oxford University
    Press. ★★★★☆
Although this book deals with perennial philosophical problems, the introduction in particular
provides a good account as to why thinking critically is so important to the lives of both human
individuals and wider human societies.

Hare, W (2001) Bertrand Russell on critical thinking. *Journal of Thought* 36, 1: 7–16. (Can be
    found at www.criticalthinking.org/articles/bertrand-russell.cfm. Accessed July 2008.) ★★★☆☆
This is a really thorough online text that outlines the British philosopher Bertrand Russell's
understanding of the concept of critical thinking and it provided much of the material for the latter
two figures in this chapter. One of the best aspects of this analysis of critical thinking is the focus
upon the attributes or dispositions required to think critically.

Johnson-Laird, P (2006) *How We Reason.* Oxford: Oxford University Press. ★★★★☆
Although this comprises over 400 pages of text and another hundred or so of notes and references, it
is a beautifully written book that is so much more than a book on critical thinking. In fact, as it is
written from a background of cognitive psychology it should be seen as an interesting and accessible
popular science book rather than the typically dry critical thinking textbook. As such, in providing
background knowledge in how our brains are able to think critically (or in many cases, fail to do so)
it is highly recommended.

Moon, J (2008) *Critical Thinking: An Exploration of Theory and Practice.* London: Routledge.
    ★★☆☆☆
This book is written from a pedagogical perspective that reflects upon the relationship between
critical thinking and education. As a whole, the consideration of the concept of critical thinking
takes a more descriptive than philosophical analysis in that it highlights the ambiguity and
confusion surrounding the term that is often perceived by a 'lay' population; as such there is little
attempt at the conceptual analysis that would be undertaken by more philosophical approaches to
the subject. Whilst the reflective style of language contained throughout may appeal to some
readers, others might find it rather puerile.

Paul, RW and Elder, L (2002) *Critical Thinking: Tools for Taking Charge of Your Professional and
    Personal Life.* Upper Saddle River, NJ: FT Press. ★★☆☆☆
This is quite a weighty tome and contains a lot of information; although some of it seems heavily
concentrated on reinforcing the same points and the language can be perceived as occasionally
patronising. Its primary focus is upon self-reflection in enabling the reader to understand and
acknowledge where they lie on the critical thinking scale. It attempts to get the reader to refine their
thinking skills in a more implicit way than other critical thinking books.

Thomson, A (1999) *Critical Reasoning in Ethics: A Practical Introduction.* London: Routledge.
    ★★★★☆

Following Thomson's other work on critical reasoning, this book focuses specifically on analysing ethical arguments and their underlying value judgements. It covers much of the foundational issues in argument evaluation but also provides a really useful framework for making decisions on ethical matters as well as an overview to some basic ethical theories.

Answers to Learning Activities

Learning Activity 1.1
All of the following statements are the types of claim or evidence that is assessed throughout this book. The answers provide signposts for where discussion on related issues is discussed further.

a) The Ukrainian Oleksandr Petriv broke the 25m rapid fire pistol shooting record in the Beijing 2008 Olympics. – *This statement could be verified by direct or indirect observation, e.g. either you could have observed the event yourself or you could refer to credible sources of Olympic records to determine whether this is true or not (see the section on evidence in Chapter 4).*

b) Water polo is a sport. – *This is a definitional statement, that is, part of understanding the activity of water polo means recognising it as a sport (and therefore everything that sport entails). However, the definition of sport is a contested concept and so it is open to negotiation and change (see analytical and synthetic statements in Chapter 4).*

c) Hitler attempted to use the 1936 Berlin Olympics as a vehicle to promote his Nazi ideology. – *This statement can be evaluated in the light of previous historical events and interpretations of these events. Although it is believed to be true by a general consensus it is still a statement of judgement (see assessing the credibility of sources in Chapter 4).*

d) In 100 years time, Formula One racing will no longer exist. – *This is a statement of opinion and a prediction of future events. There may be reasonable argument to support this claim but it is open to discussion and debate (see Chapters 2 and 3).*

e) Muscles require adenosine triphosphate to function. – *This is a scientific statement that is based upon the method of induction (see inductive arguments in Chapter 5).*

f) Boxing should be taught as part of the PE curriculum in every secondary school. – *This is a statement of value as denoted by the word 'should'. It cannot be verified by any evidence though a reasonable and rational case could be made to support it (see this chapter and the 'is-ought' fallacy in Chapter 6).*

Learning Activity 1.2
The answers to these questions are up to you but they do require critical thought.

Learning Activity 1.3
a) I don't enjoy having to train in the cold, wet and dark. – *This is a statement of preference.*

b) Games played on artificial turf are much faster than those played on grass. – *There may be exceptions to this but it is likely that objective evidence would support this statement and therefore it would be considered a statement of fact.*

c) The levels of financial investment required to compete in the Olympic Games means it is not a fair competition. – *This is a statement of reason as it deals with the contested concept of fairness.*

d) There is nothing more exciting than watching the Grand National directly from the stands. – *This is a statement of preference.*

e) Levels of obesity are rising in all developed, Westernised countries. – *If there is an agreed definition of 'obesity' then this is a statement of fact.*

f) Sport is a valuable social tool to enhance the lives of disaffected young people. – *This is a statement of reason as it focuses on the concept of a 'good life' and the value of sport.*

g) The rectus abdominis, transversus abdominis, external oblique and internal oblique are the four muscles that make up the stomach muscles. – *This is a statement of fact.*

h) The England women's cricket team should have received the BBC Sports Personality 'Team of the Year' award in 2009. – *This is a statement of reason as it is making a judgement.*

Learning Activity 1.4

Suggested answers:

a) Wolves won 36–15 last weekend. – *This is a statement of fact and can be verified by direct or indirect observation.*

b) Richard will be selected to compete in Hong Kong. – *This appears to be a statement of fact but is much weaker than the previous one since it refers to an event in the future. It is also dependent on who is making the judgement and upon what basis. However, as it is phrased, with the use of 'will be', it is a statement of fact rather than value.*

c) The goalkeeper made a huge error by moving off his goal line. – *This is a moral judgement (i.e. stating the keeper made a mistake) in that it provides an assessment of an event. It is therefore a statement of value.*

d) You should rest if you want to recover quickly from your injury. – *This is a hypothetical imperative, as it says if you want X then you should do Y. Although it provides a recommendation, if we accept the evidence that rest speeds recovery then it is arguably a statement of fact rather than value. (See Chapter 3 for 'if-then' arguments.)*

e) The league begins on 14 September. – *This is a statement of fact and can be verified by records.*

f) You should go to training. – *In contrast to (d), this is a statement of value as it provides a moral recommendation; simply that you ought to do X. It is called a categorical imperative.*

g) You should support Liverpool over Everton. – *This is a statement of value similar to the previous.*

h) Ashley took the wrong route in the cross-country race. – *The word 'wrong' here is not used in a moral sense as there was a specific route that was designated for the race which Ashley didn't follow. It is therefore a statement of fact.*

i) Ethan was wrong to use steroids. – *This is a statement of value as it provides a moral judgement.*

Learning Activity 1.5

a) Critical thinking involves asking relevant questions and questioning assumptions. – *TRUE.*

b) There are some areas in the study of sport that don't require the ability to think critically. – *FALSE (Critical thinking is necessary in all areas of the academic study of sport).*

c) Critical thinking is about reaching the correct answer. – *FALSE (Often there is no 'correct' or 'right' answer; it is about providing a justification for your claim and attempting to persuade others of its reasonableness).*

d) The skills required in critical thinking are those required in graduate-level employment. – *TRUE.*

e) The ability to think critically requires the courage of openness, honesty and courage. – *TRUE.*

f) Statements of reason are those that can be defended and justified. – *TRUE.*

g) Value judgements are simply an expression of opinion. – *FALSE (Value judgements may be based on fundamental preferences or values but still need to be justified).*

h) The skills of critical thought can be easily acquired. – *FALSE (These skills require ongoing practice and perfection).*

Chapter 2
What is an argument?

Learning Objectives

This chapter will help you:

- understand what constitutes an argument;
- appreciate the relationship between critical thinking and arguments;
- recognise types of words that indicate that a reason or conclusion is being offered;
- identify components of arguments – in particular, *reasons, conclusions* and *intermediate conclusions* in longer passages of argument.

Introduction

Imagine that, in a competition tie-breaker to win tickets to a sporting event of your choosing, you are asked to fill in the blanks of the following statement:

.... is my favourite sport because ....

This, in its most basic of form, is an argument. You are making a claim (for your favourite sport) and providing a reason to support this claim. This is what this chapter is about.

The previous chapter provided an overview of the concept of critical thinking and why it is important to you and your studies. To summarise, thinking critically entails:

- *Being reasonable.*
- *Being reflective.*
- *Focusing upon what to believe or do.*

(List adapted from Ennis, 1996)

Underpinning these is the assumption that one values *getting things right*. It is impossible to be a critical thinker without the dispositions of honesty, courage, patience and openness. Yet whilst such dispositions and virtues provide the foundation, the mark of a good critical thinker is an ability to assess arguments. When I mention to my students that critical thinking is about being good at arguing, some become despondent and reply that they don't like arguing. They picture an argument as a fight, aggressive confrontation or altercation; whereas an academic argument is much more sober, considered, rational and reasonable. Those involved in arguments in the academic sense are less concerned with winning and more with reaching the best possible conclusion, hence the relationship to those qualities of a good critical thinker (see Figures 2.1 and 2.2).

The standard definition of an argument is a *conclusion (or claim) that is supported by reasons (or premises)* (Figure 2.3).

Reasons are statements that provide evidence or supply a definition. Essentially, they tell you why something ought to be believed to be true. For example, in the previous chapter, I offered several reasons to support the statement that critical thinking is an important skill to develop. The reasons that were given were: it enables us to reach our potential; it helps us decide what course of action to take to reach a specific outcome; and it is the type of skill that is required for achieving the top grades at university.

A conclusion is the main judgement reached in an argument. It can be a recommendation, interpretation or verdict. Essentially, conclusions direct or justify action.

An argument IS:

Sober

Considered   Rational

Reasonable

Figure 2.1.

An argument is NOT:

A shouting match

A personal vendetta

An irrational rant

Figure 2.2.

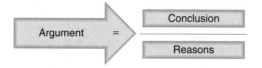

Argument = Conclusion / Reasons

Figure 2.3.

Case Study 2.1
What are reasons and conclusions? An analogy

Imagine a conclusion being a Formula One racing car and the reasons being the engineering and technology that underpin it. Whilst all the cars might look similar when they line up on the starting grid, the cars that perform the best are the ones that have the strongest and most reliable technology. In the same way, conclusions might be supported by a number of reasons, but the best arguments are the ones that are founded on resilient and trustworthy evidence.

Identifying arguments

The standard definition of an argument is a conclusion that is supported by a reason (or reasons). Therefore, an argument cannot be a singular statement, e.g. 'The argument that boxing is immoral.' A conclusion might state that 'boxing is immoral' but for it to become an argument it must be supported by reasons, such as, 'Boxing is the deliberate intent to harm another person' or 'Boxing is violent'. Also, remember that an argument isn't the same thing as a quarrel or a fight. Even if you are making a claim that is controversial or not held by others, it doesn't mean it is an argument (in the academic sense). In the same vein, an argument isn't a simple, but essentially pointless, contradiction, e.g. 'Yes it is.' 'No, it isn't.' 'Yes, it is . . .' etc. Rather, it is generally accepted that an academic argument, no matter how passionately held, is a rational and logical expression of ideas and not an emotional outburst.

Other things that aren't arguments

All of the following examples are not arguments because they do not contain conclusions or claims that are supported by reasons.

- *Descriptions of events*, such as match reports:

  A ferociously fast-paced game saw the Galactic Bolts overcome the Teddington Tigers, with Michelle Rowe scoring a hat-trick. Next weekend the Bolts will face top of the table Islington Rapters which will be a rematch of last year's cup final which saw the Rapters winning in extra time.

- *Explanations or instructions* on how to complete a manoeuvre or skill:

  Start standing up, with your back to the mat or spotter and your arms by your ears. Swing your arms down and behind you, while bending your knees. Swing your arms back up and jump as high as you can. Keep your head neutral – looking straight ahead. Your jump should go upward and slightly backward, onto the mat or the spotter. Your arms should stay straight.

- *Expressions of emotion* that may indicate a judgement or conclusion but which do not provide any supporting reasons:

  'We had a blatant penalty and the referee bottled it. If it's not a level playing field and if we don't get the decisions, blatant, important decisions then what is the point of turning up?' vented Jones following United's 3–1 defeat against Rangers.

- *Unsupported claims* that provide no reasons to suggest the claim ought to be accepted:
  It's obvious that England will never win the World Cup again.
- *Seductive or emotive language* that aims to persuade the audience to accept the claim through flattery and adulation:
  Our athletes are underfunded. With your financial support, you can be part of helping our Olympic hopefuls to achieve gold.
- *Threatening language* that suggests non-acceptance of the claim will lead to negative consequences:
  T.J. Smith's sponsorship deal ends at the end of the season. If it isn't renewed, it will put the club in severe financial hardship, which will mean we will lose our best players.

It may be that some passages seem to be providing an argument but the argument is implied rather than made explicit (see Chapter 5 for more information on this). When assessing a passage, it is useful to first identify what is actually being said, and then later in your evaluation reconstruct it in order to give an account of what could have been said in order to make it into an actual argument. In example f), below, that asks people to be involved in the campaign to get lacrosse into the Olympics, an argument is not being made. It is simply a request. However, it would not be unreasonable to suppose that the person making the request believes that lacrosse *should* be part of the Olympics and would be able to provide a reason to support this claim. However, it must be remembered that this argument has not been stated but is merely presupposed. When identifying arguments, it is important to look closely at what has actually been said rather than what *could* have been said. It is my experience that some students tend to neglect this difference especially when it is on a subject or issue that they feel passionately about.

Learning Activity 2.1

In the following passages, decide whether an argument is being made. For those examples that are arguments, attempt to identify (1) the reason(s) and (2) the conclusion. For those that are not arguments, decide which type of non-argument, as illustrated in the previous section, they fall under.

a) In rugby, a ruck is when two or more players from each side are engaged in contact over the ball whereas a maul is when two or more players from each side are engaged in contact with the ball.
b) Physical education is a way of combating obesity. As obesity is becoming more of a problem in society, schools should spend much more time teaching physical education.
c) 'Uwe Proske (Monash University) outlined the basic anatomy and function of muscle spindles in relation to disturbed proprioception after exercise and the role in sports

injuries. Muscle spindles have two different roles: to provide signals for the sense of position and movement (conscious) and to provide input to motor neurons as part of the stretch reflex (unconscious)' (Hume and Paton, 2008).

d) Disaffected youth can find purpose and meaning to their lives through sport. However, funding for this area has been drastically cut. The government says it is serious about reducing the amount of disaffected young people so it should increase the funding for these sports projects.

e) Exercise physiology assesses the effect of exercise (activity that enhances or maintains physical fitness) on the constitutive parts of the body, in particular, the nervous system, the cardiovascular system, the pulmonary system and the musculoskeletal system.

f) Please join our campaign to get lacrosse in the Olympics. We need as many signatures as possible.

g) The current drug testing procedures violate the athlete's right to privacy. Therefore athletes should not be subjected to drug testing.

h) 'Abandonments offer grounds for wider debate. Artificial watering at the heart of a problem that is causing dissent and ill-feeling among racing's constituents' (Hislop, 2008).

Looking closely at reasons and conclusions

As illustrated throughout this chapter, an argument is a conclusion that is supported by reasons. It is therefore important to be able to distinguish which is the conclusion and which are the reasons.

Conclusions are supported by reasons but may not necessarily be stated at the end of the argument; in other words, they may not necessarily 'conclude' the statement. Sometimes, conclusions are given at the outset. So, how do you know which is which? One answer is given by Cottrell (2005) who states, 'A conclusion is usually a deduction, which draws together the argument, and makes a reasoned assumption about how to interpret the reasons' (p46). Another way of gauging which is the reason and which is the conclusion is that the conclusion is often a recommendation that follows from (for instance, saying something should or ought to happen), or an interpretation of, information given in another statement.

Consider the following examples,

- *Pedometers are useful motivational tools for encouraging people to exercise more. They should be given to those who lead fairly sedentary lives such as office workers, and also to children to get them into good habits.*
- *Susie has had a successful netball career. She has over 50 caps for England and has played in the National Premier league for over 15 years.*

In the first example, the reason is given first and the conclusion last, whereas in the second example (see Figure 2.4), the conclusion is given first and the reasons that support the conclusion are given afterwards (see Figure 2.5).

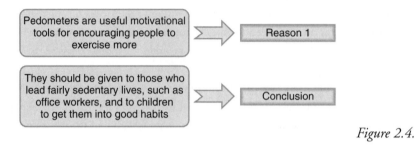

Figure 2.4.

The second part of the statement, 'They should . . .', denotes a recommendation that because one thing is the case, i.e. 'Pedometers are useful motivational tools . . .' another thing should follow.

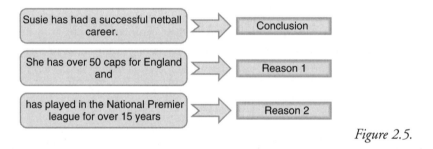

Figure 2.5.

Here, the conclusion is an interpretation of two 'facts' about the world, i.e. 50 caps for England and 15 years of playing in the Premiership is akin to a successful netball career. We will look more closely at the structure of arguments, and particularly whether the arguments are good ones or not, in the following chapters.

Learning Activity 2.2

For the following examples, try to work out which is the statement (conclusion) that the author is trying to persuade you to accept, and which is the reason they are giving in support of this assertion. Bear in mind that they might not necessarily be good arguments even though they contain a reason and a conclusion.

a) That can't be Doncaster training. They only train on Tuesdays and Thursdays.
b) Children's habits are set at an early age. It is important to ensure all primary school teachers are given training in physical education.

c) George hasn't been able to go windsurfing for the past year. Her back still isn't fully healed.

d) Falmouth hockey team lost 3–0 on Saturday. Many of their best players were away with county training.

e) Parkour is supposed to be non-competitive. Those that have entered the national championships have sold out.

f) Newcastle United supporters want to be considered as a political party in order to campaign to reinstate their manager. Only political and religious movements are allowed to distribute leaflets without prior permission.

g) Children need to realise how important fitness is as part of a healthy life. The government should prioritise PE as a school subject.

Reason and conclusion indicators

If you found it difficult to decide which part of the examples are reasons and which are conclusions, there are some words that are helpful in identifying which are which; these are called reason and conclusion indicators (Figure 2.6).

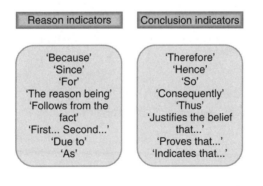

Figure 2.6.

If you are unsure as to which proposition is the reason and which is the conclusion then it can be helpful to insert one of these indicator words. For example: 'That can't be Doncaster training *because* they only train on Tuesdays and Thursdays.'

If the word 'because' (as a reason indicator) was given prior to the conclusion, it would be obvious that the argument has been misunderstood as the sentence would sound odd: '*Because* that can't be Doncaster training, they only train on Tuesdays and Thursdays.' You can even rearrange the order of the clauses to test which indicator words give the most sense: '*Because* they only train on Tuesdays and Thursdays, that can't be Doncaster training.' Or: 'They only train on Tuesdays and Thursdays *so* that can't be Doncaster training.'

Identifying reasons and conclusions in longer passages of argument

In longer passages of argument, reasons and conclusions may be more difficult to identify as they change their nature depending on which aspect you are focusing on at the time. For instance, a conclusion to one part of the argument may provide a reason to support a later claim. In this case, we would call the initial conclusion an *intermediate conclusion* as it forms the initial part of an argument that needs to be accepted before any later conclusions are presented.

The case studies and figures below indicate how longer pieces of argument can be broken down into their constitutive parts, and which statements act as a reason supporting one claim whilst being a conclusion for another. In both case studies there is additional information, supporting evidence and acknowledgement of counter-argument, but the figures attempt to strip down to the bare bones of the argument being made.

Case Study 2.2

'Some of the best things in life don't translate very well to TV . . . So it is with swimming, which, despite the best efforts of roof cam, slow-mo-droplet cam and underwater-perv cam, remains an unrelentingly linear TV experience . . . The most obvious problem here is that for the TV viewer, swimming is basically just bobbing heads . . . In fact, long stretches of it were a bit like being beaten around the head with a repeatedly bobbing rubberised skull-cap. Why are there so many races? In athletics, after the men's 100 metres, nobody says, "OK, Usain, now turn around and run it backwards and we'll give you another gold medal. Then run it in a slightly odd-mannered way where you flap your arms and we'll call it the 100m Men's Nerdy Flail. Another gold right there". The race overload is particularly self-defeating as on the small screen the best bits of swimming are the bits in between, the bits where there is no swimming.'

[Ronay, 2009]

In this example (Figure 2.7), the author attempts to argue that swimming doesn't work well on television (Conclusion 2). The reason given to support this conclusion is that it is a linear experience

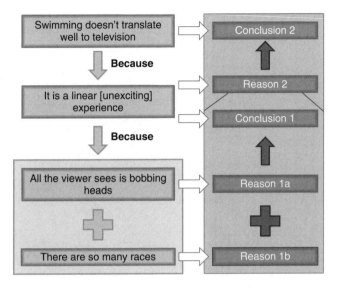

Figure 2.7.

(despite all the additional television technology that is used) (Reason 2). Here, the use of the term 'linear' in this context has been interpreted to essentially mean 'unexciting' or 'uninteresting'. This point then becomes an intermediate claim (Conclusion 1) that is supported by the reasons: all the viewer sees is bobbing heads (Reason 1a), and that there is an overload of races (Reason 1b).

Case Study 2.3

Bristol's losing run at the beginning of the season was put down to the fact that they were made to wear their away shirts. These white shirts showed up more noticeably than darker colours under floodlights and meant that the referee was more likely to spot infringements made by Bristol players than infringements made by the opposition, hence Bristol conceded more penalties. This greater penalty count cost them games.

In this example (Figure 2.8), the final conclusion (Conclusion 3) is that Bristol lost. The reason for them losing is that they conceded more penalties (Reason 3) (with the added unstated assumption that teams that concede more penalties lose). This then becomes an intermediate conclusion (Conclusion 2) that is supported by the reason that the referee spotted more infringements (Reason 2) (with the unstated assumption that spotted infringements leads to conceding penalties). The reasons that support this intermediate conclusion (Conclusion 1) are that Bristol wore white shirts (Reason 1a) and white shirts are more visible than dark shirts under floodlights (Reason 1b) (with the unstated premise that they were playing under floodlights at the time).

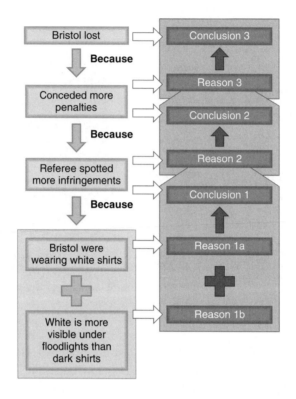

Figure 2.8.

Learning Activity 2.4

For the following passages, attempt to identify the argument that is being made and any intermediate conclusions that act as reasons to support other conclusions.

a) Steve believes that his chances of winning an Olympic Gold medal are not over yet despite the fact that he will be in his late thirties by the time his next opportunity arrives. He said, 'I am training harder than ever nowadays and I feel more comfortable with my performance, both physically and psychologically. There is no reason to suppose that my body will not be able to perform at the highest level when the next Olympics comes around.'

b) 'Ascot officials have acted to prevent the Royal racecourse being associated with the sale of ex-racehorses for meat for human consumption. Their contracted auctioneers, Brightwells, have been told to tighten their sales conditions to prevent any such trade taking place. Horses can fetch up to £650 when slaughtered for meat to be sold on the continent but the minimum sale price at Brightwells is as low as £300, raising fears that "meat men" might be attracted to the Ascot Sales. The minimum sales price at Doncaster and Newmarket is much higher at £500. But buyers of horses priced between £300 and

£800 will now face a life ban from Brightwells if unable to provide evidence of what a horse is doing, or where it is living, six months after it was purchased' (Radford, 2008).

c) 'It has been suggested that diet may affect behaviour. In some ancient cultures certain foods were thought to have magical qualities capable of giving special powers of strength, courage, health, happiness and well-being. It is possible that some food constituents may affect the synthesis of brain neurotransmitters and thus modify brain functions. It is therefore important to integrate dietary effects on brain chemicals into our wider understanding of human behaviour' (Eastwood, 2003, p4).

d) 'Recent evidence demonstrates that increases in blood levels of potassium stimulate the carotid bodies and promote an increase in ventilation. Since blood potassium levels rise during exercise due to a net potassium efflux from the contracting muscle, some investigators have suggested that potassium may play a role in regulating ventilation during exercise' (Powers and Howley, 2007, p221).

e) 'At present, certain areas of sport get substantial funds through tobacco sponsorship. The great irony is that a physical activity like sport should be supported by such a physically destructive product. The argument in favour of tobacco sponsorship has always been that some sports depend on it. This argument is somewhat spurious. Even cricket is now getting as much help from the finance houses and insurance firms as it is from tobacco. If money has to go from tobacco to sport let it be through a levy on tobacco company profit' (Whannel, 2008, p103).

Even though the previous case study and the learning activities are only single paragraphs, they illustrate that the structure of arguments can be quite complex and the constitutive parts difficult to identify. The structure of arguments and ways of depicting them will be considered in more detail in the next chapter.

Test Your Understanding

Learning Activity 2.5

State whether the following statements are true or false.

a) The ability to construct and deconstruct arguments is a key skill in critical thinking.
b) An argument is a strongly held opinion.
c) An argument needs to state all viewpoints.
d) An argument is a claim that is supported by reasons.
e) Arguments are generally used in an attempt to persuade others that something is the case.

••• ▶

f) Arguments always contain reason and conclusion indicator words.

g) 'Therefore', 'Thus', 'Consequently' and 'So' are examples of conclusion indicators.

h) 'As', 'Since', 'Because' and 'For' are examples of reason indicators.

i) Reasons and conclusions are interchangeable.

j) Sometimes conclusions in one part of an argument can function as reasons in another.

Chapter Review

What is an argument?

An argument is a *claim that is supported by reasons*, or (in other words) *premise(s) leading to a conclusion*.

What types of things aren't arguments?

Reports, descriptions, definitions and unsupported claims are not arguments. Expressions of emotion, threats and seduction are only arguments if they contain a reason and a (related) conclusion.

What is a reason or premise?

A reason is a proposition given in attempt to persuade someone to believe something (a claim or conclusion) is true.

What is a conclusion or claim?

A conclusion is the main judgement given in an argument.

What is an intermediate conclusion?

A reason can also act as an intermediate conclusion if it is being supported by another reason.

Further Reading

Ennis, R (1996) *Critical Thinking*. London: Prentice-Hall. ★★★★★

This is by far the most definitive resource for critical thinking that I have come across and is thoroughly recommended. Although the explanations are comprehensive and well written, the scope and depth covered can be quite daunting for a first-time student in critical thinking (I first used it as a third-year undergraduate and found it quite overwhelming). Nevertheless, it provides a wealth of exercises and examples, a comprehensive glossary, and is unlikely to be surpassed as the bible for critical thinking in the near future. The more I read it, the more I appreciate its value.

Garnham, A and Oakhill, J (1994) *Thinking and Reasoning*. Oxford: Blackwell. ★★★☆☆
Although this is not a textbook, it does cover many of the usual themes in critical thinking, such as deduction, induction, formal logic, syllogisms, statistical reasoning, game reasoning, creativity and everyday reasoning. Written from a psychological perspective, it contains lots of interesting theory and evidence regarding our abilities as humans to think. Perhaps particularly of note is their claim that 'generally, attempts to teach people to think leave the impression that learning to think is a long and time-consuming process – rather like learning any complex skill, in fact', which eloquently suggests the need for these types of texts and courses.

Govier, T (2010) *A Practical Study of Argument* (seventh edition). Belmont: Wadsworth. ★★★★★
When a book reaches a seventh edition, it is likely that it is both popular and that its author has a genuine desire to improve and update it. Indeed, this text is a valuable resource that covers all aspects of critical thinking in a sufficient but also accessible depth. Not only does it contain exercises within the textbook, but there is also an additional electronic resource and an instructor's manual which contains further guidance and answers to exercises.

Nosich, GM (2009) *Learning to Think Things Through: A Guide to Critical Thinking Across the Curriculum* (third edition). Upper Saddle River, NJ: Pearson Prentice-Hall. ★★★☆☆
This textbook is designed to be interdisciplinary but aims also to provide students with the tools for analysing arguments within a specific discipline; and in this respect its commentary on understanding the vocabularies of disciplines is useful and something that isn't explicitly covered in other books on the subject. It closely follows Paul and Elder's conception of, and models for, critical thinking and also provides many reflective exercises to consolidate the ideas presented.

Paul, R and Elder, L (2004) *The Miniature Guide to Critical Thinking: Concepts and Tools* (fourth edition). Dillon Beach, CA: The Foundation for Critical Thinking. ★★★☆☆
As a miniature guide this packs a lot of information into a small amount of space. It is one of twenty miniature resources on critical thinking (others include titles such as Strategic Thinking, Ethical Reasoning, and Critical and Creative Thinking) but provides a useful and easily accessible overview. As it is self-published by The Foundation for Critical Thinking, it isn't particularly flashy or as professionally laid out as other publications (there is a range of font sizes depending on the information required to fit on a page, for example) but it is a cheap and handy resource if you just need reminders of the central tenets of critical thought. There is also a wealth of additional material on the foundation's website, www.criticalthinking.org (accessed November 2009).

Weston, A (2000) *A Rulebook for Arguments* (third edition). Cambridge: Hackett Publishing Company. ★★★☆☆
As noted in the preface, this is a rulebook not a textbook and aims to provide reminders to students in following the rules of good argument. Although it doesn't provide any exercises for students, it is written in a clear, engaging and accessible way. This means it is useful as a handy resource to delve into when you've just got a few minutes to spare whilst waiting for a bus for instance.

Answers to Learning Activities

Learning Activity 2.1

a) In rugby, a ruck is when two or more players from each side are engaged in contact over the ball whereas a maul is when two or more players from each side are engaged in contact with the ball. *– This is not an argument. It is merely a definition.*

b) Physical education is a way of combating obesity. As obesity is becoming more of a problem in society, schools should spend much more time teaching physical education. *– This is an argument. The conclusion is that 'schools should spend much more time teaching physical education' and the supporting reasons are that 'obesity is becoming more of a problem in society' and that 'physical education is a way of combating obesity'.*

c) 'Uwe Proske (Monash University) outlined the basic anatomy and function of muscle spindles in relation to disturbed proprioception after exercise and the role in sports injuries. Muscle spindles have two different roles: to provide signals for the sense of position and movement (conscious) and to provide input to motor neurons as part of the stretch reflex (unconscious)' (Hume and Paton, 2008). *– This is not an argument. It is a description of an event and an explanation of a process.*

d) Disaffected youth can find purpose and meaning to their lives through sport. However, funding for this area has been drastically cut. The government says it is serious about reducing the amount of disaffected young people so it should increase the funding for these sports projects. *– This is an argument, although it is slightly more complex than previous ones. The conclusion is that 'the government should increase funding for sports projects' and the reasons are that 'disaffected youth can find purpose and meaning to their lives through sport' and that 'the government says it wants to reduce the amount of disaffected young people'.*

e) Exercise physiology assesses the effect of exercise (activity that enhances or maintains physical fitness) on the constitutive parts of the body, in particular, the nervous system, the cardiovascular system, the pulmonary system and the musculoskeletal system. *– This is not an argument. It is merely a description.*

f) Please join our campaign to get lacrosse in the Olympics. We need as many signatures as possible. *– This is not an argument. It is a plea to persuade people to act in a particular way.*

g) The current drug testing procedures violate the athlete's right to privacy. Therefore athletes should not be subjected to drug testing. *– This is an argument. The conclusion is that 'athletes should not be subjected to drug testing' and the reason is that 'the current drug testing procedures violate the athlete's right to privacy'.*

h) 'Abandonments offer grounds for wider debate. Artificial watering at the heart of a problem that is causing dissent and ill-feeling among racing's constituents' (Hislop, 2008). *– This is not an argument. Two claims are stated but no reasons are given in support of these claims. However, as it is a newspaper headline, there is the assumption that the proceeding story will offer reasons to support these claims.*

Learning Activity 2.2

a) That can't be Doncaster training (*Conclusion*). They only train on Tuesdays and Thursdays (*Reason*).

b) Children's habits are set at an early age (*Reason*). It is important to ensure all primary school teachers are given training in physical education (*Conclusion*).

c) George hasn't been able to go windsurfing for the past year (*Conclusion*). Her back still isn't fully healed (*Reason*).

d) Falmouth hockey team lost 3–0 on Saturday (*Conclusion*). Many of their best players were away with county training (*Reason*).

e) Parkour is supposed to be non-competitive (*Reason*). Those that have entered the national championships have sold out (*Conclusion*).

f) Newcastle United supporters want to be considered as a political party in order to campaign to reinstate their manager (*Conclusion*). Only political and religious movements are allowed to distribute leaflets without prior permission (*Reason*).

g) Children need to realise how important fitness is as part of a healthy life (*Reason*). The government should prioritise PE as a school subject (*Conclusion*).

Learning Activity 2.3

Suggested answers:

a) That can't be Doncaster training *because/as/since* they only train on Tuesdays and Thursdays.

b) Children's habits are set at an early age *so/therefore/thus* it is important to ensure all primary school teachers are given training in physical education.

c) George hasn't been able to go windsurfing for the past year *because* her back still isn't fully healed.

d) Falmouth hockey team lost 3–0 on Saturday *as* many of their best players were away with county training.

e) Parkour is supposed to be non-competitive *so* those that have entered the national championships have sold out.

f) Newcastle United supporters want to be considered as a political party in order to campaign to reinstate their manager *for the reason that* only political and religious movements are allowed to distribute leaflets without prior permission.

g) Children need to realise how important fitness is as part of a healthy life, *therefore* the government should prioritise PE as a school subject.

Learning Activity 2.4

The suggested answers below (Figures 2.9 to 2.13) depict the most straightforward form of the argument that is being presented. Many of the examples contain added assumptions (see Chapter 5) that could have been embedded to form more complex arguments.

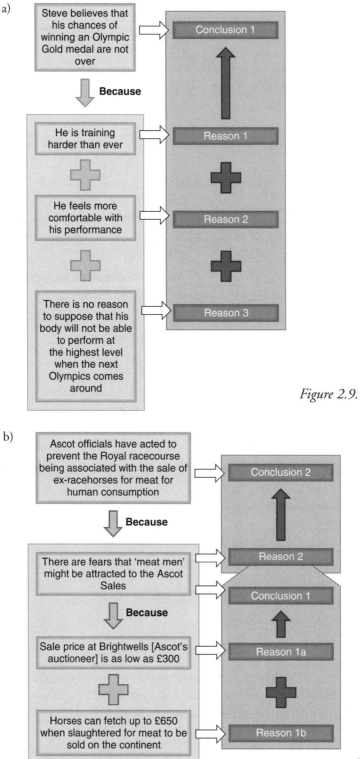

a)

Steve believes that his chances of winning an Olympic Gold medal are not over

Because

He is training harder than ever

He feels more comfortable with his performance

There is no reason to suppose that his body will not be able to perform at the highest level when the next Olympics comes around

Conclusion 1

Reason 1

Reason 2

Reason 3

Figure 2.9.

b)

Ascot officials have acted to prevent the Royal racecourse being associated with the sale of ex-racehorses for meat for human consumption

Because

There are fears that 'meat men' might be attracted to the Ascot Sales

Because

Sale price at Brightwells [Ascot's auctioneer] is as low as £300

Horses can fetch up to £650 when slaughtered for meat to be sold on the continent

Conclusion 2

Reason 2

Conclusion 1

Reason 1a

Reason 1b

Figure 2.10.

c)

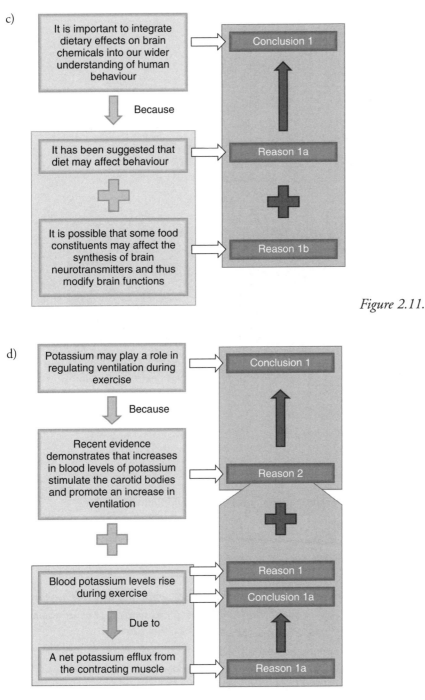

Figure 2.11.

d)

Figure 2.12.

e)

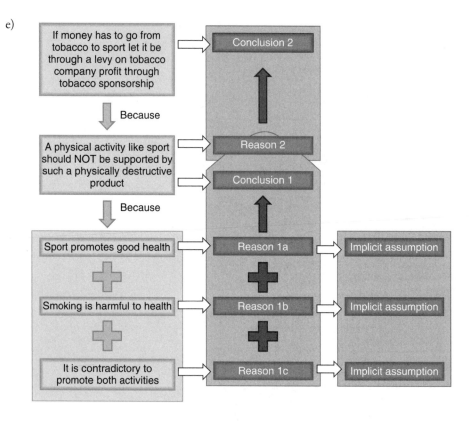

Figure 2.13.

Learning Activity 2.5

a) The ability to construct and deconstruct arguments is a key skill in critical thinking – *TRUE.*

b) An argument is a strongly held opinion – *FALSE (There is no requirement that the person making an argument believes it to either be a good argument and/or a true one. Also, an argument is much more than an opinion).*

c) An argument needs to state all viewpoints – *FALSE (A longer argument may take into account contrary positions and show how they are insufficient, but as long as an argument provides reasons for its own claim, it doesn't need to state other viewpoints).*

d) An argument is a claim that is supported by reasons – *TRUE.*

e) Arguments are generally used in an attempt to persuade others that something is the case – *TRUE.*

f) Arguments always contain reason and conclusion indicator words – *FALSE (Whilst many arguments do contain reason and conclusion indicators in order to make it clear that an argument is being made, it is not a necessary requirement and sometimes arguments are given without them).*

g) 'Therefore', 'Thus', 'Consequently' and 'So' are examples of conclusion indicators – *TRUE*.

h) 'As', 'Since', 'Because' and 'For' are examples of reason indicators – *TRUE*.

i) Reasons and conclusions are interchangeable – *FALSE (Whilst conclusions can act as reasons in a later argument, reasons and conclusions have different functions).*

j) Sometimes conclusions in one part of an argument can function as reasons in another – *TRUE*.

Chapter 3
Evaluating an argument's structure: deductive arguments

Learning Objectives

This chapter will help you:

- understand how to assess an argument based on its structure;
- recognise the logical form of basic arguments and syllogisms;
- assess the deductive validity of basic arguments;
- use diagrams to represent some forms of argument.

The previous chapter outlined what makes something an argument (as opposed to an instruction or expression of emotion) but with some of the examples provided, you may not have been convinced of their quality as good arguments. This chapter will consider what makes an argument a good (or bad) one and will, in turn, emphasise ways of making arguments better. Over the next few chapters, we will look at two aspects of arguments: the *structure* (the relationship between the premises and the conclusion) and the *content* (the truth of the premises). This chapter will deal specifically with the structure of arguments.

Deductive reasoning

One way of deciding whether an argument is a good one is to determine whether the reasons necessarily lead to the conclusion. This is called *deductive reasoning* and is concerned with the internal logic (the inherent structure) of the argument. These terms, and their meanings, should become more familiar to you by the end of the chapter.

Learning Activity 3.1

Humans are generally very good at solving problems and deductive reasoning is one example of this. This chapter will consider different types of deductive arguments in detail but, in order to gauge the level of your reasoning initially, try answering the questions opposite.

a) If Alice is a swimmer, and all swimmers like water, then what can we deduce about Alice?

b) All triathletes can swim, cycle and run. Oli can't swim. What can we deduce about Oli?

c) If Athavan is watching cricket, it must be a Saturday. It is a Saturday, so is there anything we can conclude about Athavan?

d) Some athletes take illegal performance-enhancing substances. Caroline is an athlete, so is there any conclusion that follows?

e) All skate-boarders have good balance. Good balance requires good core stability. What can we deduce about skate-boarders?

f) Some footballers are goalkeepers. All goalkeepers are allowed to handle the ball. What else can we deduce about some footballers?

Let us start looking at deductive reasoning by highlighting the difference between implicit and explicit arguments. Consider one of the examples from the previous chapter:

That can't be Doncaster training [conclusion] *because they only train on Tuesdays and Thursdays* [reason].

As this argument stands, there is nothing that shows how the reason leads to the conclusion (Figure 3.1). In order to make the link between the reason and the conclusion explicit, the insertion of an additional reason is required (for more on this, see the section on Assumptions in Chapter 5). For the conclusion to necessarily follow the reason, an additional reason would be added that states 'today is neither a Tuesday nor a Thursday'. If today is a Wednesday, for example, then the link between the two statements becomes explicit and the argument is strengthened (Figure 3.2).

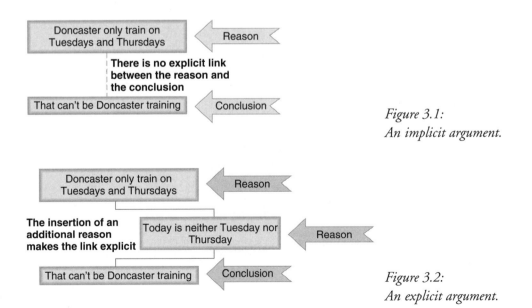

Figure 3.1:
An implicit argument.

Figure 3.2:
An explicit argument.

You may think that inserting this additional reason merely states the obvious and therefore is an unnecessary step. Yet making arguments as clear and transparent as possible is important in assessing whether they are good ones or not. And although making the link between the reason and conclusion might appear to be stating the obvious in simple arguments like this, it becomes a much more useful step in other, more unfamiliar areas of knowledge. Look at these two examples:

Carl's blood was found to contain several sets of antigens; therefore he was disqualified from the competition.

Sam was found to be wearing purple socks; therefore Carl was disqualified from the competition.

Both of these arguments have similar structural forms yet the insertion of an additional reason will show how one argument is better than the other. Neither argument makes the link between antigens or purple socks and disqualification from competition obvious. To make these arguments what is termed *deductively valid*, it requires an additional reason. For those who have knowledge about physiological blood doping tests, the link between the reason and conclusion is clear: the presence of several sets of antigens in a blood sample indicates a blood doping violation and this is a disqualificatory offence (Figure 3.3). However, the link between Sam wearing purple socks and Carl's disqualification is not clear. It may be that there is a legitimate but obscure competition rule that would render this argument valid, but if a reason cannot be found to make the argument deductively valid, then it can be considered a bad argument (Figure 3.4).

The validity of an argument is determined by whether the reasons logically lead to the conclusion and this is *one* way of assessing whether an argument is a good one (Figure 3.5).

The difference between the two examples is that the presence of an additional reason in the first example gives the argument validity, that is, it is clear how the reasons logically lead to the conclusion. In the second example, there is no (obvious) relation between Sam wearing purple socks and Carl being disqualified from the competition.

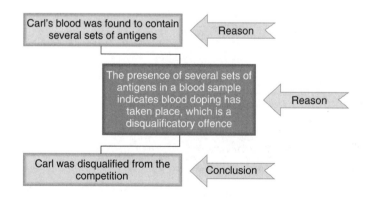

Figure 3.3.

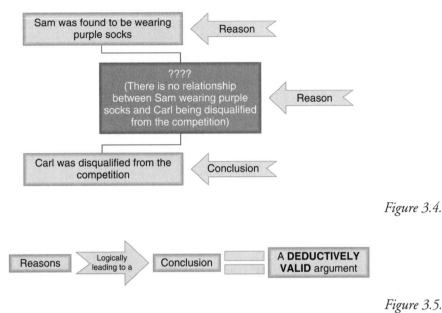

Figure 3.4.

Figure 3.5.

Learning Activity 3.2

In the arguments below, identify the reason and conclusion and insert an additional reason between the premise and the conclusion to make the argument valid.

a) Usain won the 100m sprint because he had a fast stride frequency and a long stride length.
b) Six Australasian Crusader players are to be deported due to visa irregularities.
c) Too many unforced errors led to a straight sets loss for Venus in the Toronto Cup.
d) Tamsyn showed she was knowledgeable, hard-working and could react quickly to orders. Therefore she was selected as part of the team for the Fastnet race.
e) Smith pleaded for more money to be given to GB gymnastics in order to improve results.
f) The Austrian men's doubles are the latest to withdraw from the Badminton World Championships in India amid security fears.

'If-then' arguments

Many arguments can be expressed using 'if-then' propositions. These types of arguments state that there is a logical connection between one thing happening and something else happening. This type of 'if-then' reasoning is one of the most important kinds of deductive reasoning.

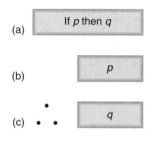

Figure 3.6.

This type of argument can be expressed as shown in Figure 3.6. In proposition a, *p* and *q* can stand for any statement that has a logical or necessary connection. In order to save time writing out complete propositions (statements) and to show the structure of arguments, letters are often used instead. The letters '*p*' and '*q*' are traditionally used, but any symbol can be used as long as it is clear to your reader which symbol stands for which proposition. For instance, *p* = 'there are several sets of antigens present' and *q* = 'Carl is guilty of blood doping.' Proposition b represents a fact or state of affairs in the world; so for example, there *are* several sets of antigens present. From propositions a and b we can deduce proposition c, that 'Carl is guilty of blood doping.' The symbol '∴' is short-hand for 'therefore'.

Let us look again at the blood doping example (Figure 3.7). This type of reasoning is useful as it shows how a conclusion can emerge from a pattern of reasoning (Figure 3.8).

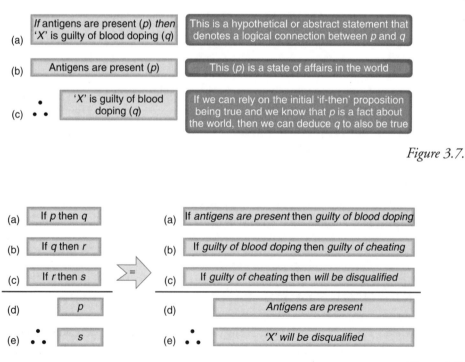

Figure 3.7.

Figure 3.8.

Deductively invalid moves (bad reasoning)

One important aspect to remember in assessing 'if-then' propositions is that they are only true in one direction. 'If *p* then *q*' doesn't mean that 'If *q* then *p*'. So whilst '*p*' being true means that '*q*' is also true, it isn't the case that '*q*' being true means that '*p*' is true. This is why no conclusion could be deduced in the cricket question in Learning Activity 3.1 (Figure 3.9).

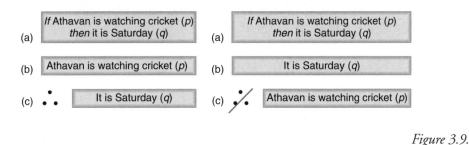

Figure 3.9.

Just because Athavan only watches cricket ('*p*') on Saturday ('*q*') (and therefore doesn't watch cricket on any other day) doesn't mean that he *must* be watching cricket if it is a Saturday. Perhaps the cricket season has finished and he watches football instead. To make this mistake is a deductively invalid move and is called *affirming the consequent*. To explain further, here is another example:

If Lucy is Welsh, she is eligible to compete for Great Britain.

Imagine there are three different possible worlds:

a) Lucy is Welsh.
b) Lucy is not Welsh.
c) Lucy is eligible to compete for Great Britain.

If the situation in world a was true, it is perfectly valid to conclude that Lucy is eligible to compete for Great Britain, since it fulfils the criteria of the 'if *p* then *q*'.

However, if the situation in world b was the case it would be deductively invalid to conclude that because Lucy is not Welsh she is not eligible to compete for Great Britain; if she was Scottish, for example, she would still be eligible to compete for Great Britain.

If the situation in world c were true, again, it is not deductively valid to conclude that Lucy is Welsh simply because she is eligible to compete for Great Britain as she could be from any of the other home nations (Figure 3.10).

The technical terms for coming to the wrong conclusions (deductive invalid arguments) exemplified in the three possibilities above are *denying the antecedent* (argument b) and *affirming the consequent* (argument c).

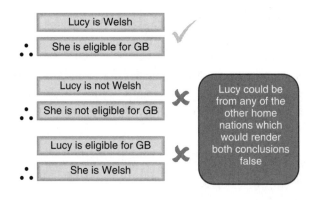

Figure 3.10.

More types of deductive arguments

The examples in Learning Activity 3.1 contained other types of deductive arguments. Let us look more closely at the first one.

If Alice is a swimmer, and all swimmers like water, then what can we deduce about Alice?

Hopefully you answered this question correctly and gave the answer 'Alice likes water.' This deductively valid argument takes the form shown in Figure 3.11.

| a) All *A*s are *B*s
b) *X* is an *A*
c) ∴ *X* is a *B* | a) All *swimmers* like *water*
b) *Alice* is a *swimmer*
c) ∴ *Alice* likes *water* |

Figure 3.11.

In this example I have deliberately kept premise a uncontroversial (that all swimmers like water) for the purposes of assessing whether the argument is a good one by being deductively valid rather than becoming sidetracked by considering whether the premises are true or not (we will deal with this aspect of arguments later in Chapters 4 and 5). To show how this argument is similar to the 'if-then' proposition and only works in one direction, look at the deductively invalid argument in Figure 3.12.

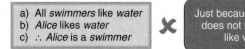

a) All *swimmers* like *water*
b) *Alice* likes *water*
c) ∴ *Alice* is a *swimmer*

Just because all swimmers like water does not mean that all people that like water are swimmers

Figure 3.12.

In contrast to the previous example, just because Alice likes water, doesn't mean that she's a swimmer. In this example, Alice could be a baby who likes to splash around in the bath or an artist who enjoys painting water scenes.

A type of deductive argument similar to the example above can be found in the skate-boarding example from Learning Activity 3.1.

All skate-boarders have good balance. Good balance requires good core stability. What can we deduce about skate-boarders?

This argument takes the form shown in Figure 3.13.

a) All *As* are *Bs*
b) All *Bs* are *Cs*
c) ∴ All *As* are *Cs*
 => =
a) All skate-boarders have good balance
b) Good balance requires good core stability
c) ∴ All skate-boarders have good core stability

Figure 3.13.

If we know that all things in one category are also in another, and we know that all things in this latter category are also in a further one, then it must be true that everything in the first category is also in the last.

This type of argument is called a syllogism and finds its origins in the ancient Greek philosophy of Aristotle. A syllogism is a particular kind of deductive argument that is formed by two premises logically leading to a conclusion. Other forms of syllogism can be found in other examples from Learning Activity 3.1. For instance:

All triathletes can swim, cycle and run. Oli can't swim. What can we deduce about Oli?

Hopefully for this question you answered, 'Oli is not a triathlete.' If we know that triathletes must be able to swim and we also know that Oli can't swim, then it logically follows that he can't be a triathlete (because if he was a triathlete then he would be able to swim). This can be expressed as shown in Figure 3.14.

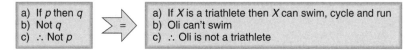

a) If *p* then *q*
b) Not *q*
c) ∴ Not *p*
 => =
a) If *X* is a triathlete then *X* can swim, cycle and run
b) Oli can't swim
c) ∴ Oli is not a triathlete

Figure 3.14.

Another syllogism can be found in this example from Learning Activity 3.1:

Some footballers are goalkeepers. All goalkeepers are allowed to handle the ball. What else can we deduce about some footballers?

The answer is that some footballers are allowed to handle the ball. This example takes the form shown in Figure 3.15.

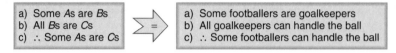

Figure 3.15.

However, contrast this argument with what seems a similar example from the same learning activity:

Some athletes take illegal performance-enhancing substances. Caroline is an athlete, so is there any conclusion that follows?

What cannot be concluded from this statement is that Caroline takes illegal performance-enhancing substances. It may be the case that she does, but without further evidence, it is equally the case that she does not. In this case, and as the saying goes, it is not fair to tar all athletes with the same brush, simply because *some* athletes take illegal substances (Figure 3.16).

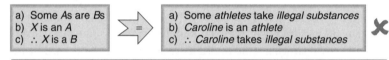

Figure 3.16.

Learning Activity 3.3

In the examples below, translate the premises into one of the logical forms that we have identified and state the conclusion (you may wish to refer to Tables 3.1 and 3.2 on p49 of this chapter).

a) All gymnasts are supple; all those who are supple have a wide range of movement, therefore . . .

b) No human has run faster than 30mph. All Olympic champions are human, therefore . . .

c) If a competitor finishes in the top three then he will automatically qualify for the final. Tom finished second, therefore . . .

d) All NBA players are men; some basketball players are NBA players, therefore . . .

e) If a coronary artery becomes blocked, it will cause a heart attack. There has been no heart attack, therefore . . .

f) The 2011 Asian Games will be hosted by either Qatar or Australia. Qatar has pulled out, therefore . . .

Classes

Sometimes it might be easier to represent the logical structure of a deductive argument by using a diagrammatic form, especially when you are dealing with classifications. Consider the following example:

a) All members of the Russian hockey team are competent ice-skaters.

b) Thomaz is a member of the Russian hockey team.

c) Therefore, Thomaz is a competent ice-skater.

We could represent this argument using the circle system in order to judge whether the conclusion is deductively valid (Figure 3.17).

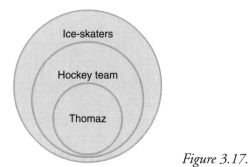

Figure 3.17.

The first premise stated that all members of the Russian hockey team are competent ice-skaters. As has been previously discussed, that does not necessarily mean that all ice-skaters are also hockey players. So being a member of the Russian hockey team is a sub-class of being a competent ice-skater (which is the largest class). The deductive conclusion that follows is that if Thomaz is a member of the Russian hockey team (a specific member of this class), it must also be true that he is a competent ice-skater (since he will also be contained in the larger class of ice-skaters). Using this system of circles allows relationships between the different classes to be easily identified and the deductive validity of arguments to be tested.

When using the circle system, if the position of the conclusion doesn't become clear by drawing the reasons then the argument is deductively invalid. We can see this in the following example:

a) All members of the Russian hockey team are competent travelling across ice.

b) All penguins are competent at travelling across ice.

c) Therefore, all penguins are members of the Russian hockey team.

If we attempt to depict this using the circle system, we find that the two premises do not dictate the location of the conclusion (Figure 3.18). The sub-class of penguins might be found within the sub-class of the Russian hockey team or it might not. This is not deducible from the premises. So we can conclude that the argument is not deductively valid.

The circle system provides a useful visual way of identifying whether the conclusion logically follows from the reasons provided. The technique to using it well is to diagram the reasons first and then note all the possibilities where the conclusion could lie. If there is only a single possibility then the argument can be considered deductively valid, if not, then it is invalid.

Figure 3.18.

Learning Activity 3.4

Use the circle system to represent the following arguments and state whether they are deductively valid or not.

a) Karen is a surfer. All surfers are able to swim. Therefore, Karen is able to swim.

b) The javelin is a field event. Athletics comprises track and field events. Therefore, the javelin is part of athletics.

c) All badminton players have quick reaction speeds. All slip fielders have quick reaction speeds. Therefore, all badminton players are slip fielders.

d) Acrophobics do not like heights. Those that do not like heights will not go base-jumping. Therefore, acrophobics will not go base-jumping.

e) Testing VO_2 max is a way of assessing physical fitness. Physical fitness can also be tested via a 20m shuttle run. Therefore, a 20m shuttle run is a way of testing VO_2 max.

f) Sport is a form of exercise. Exercise is a leisure pursuit. Therefore, sport is a leisure pursuit.

This chapter has considered one important way to verify whether an argument is a good one, in that it shows how to assess whether there is a logical relationship between the premises and the conclusion. Many arguments that are presented in the real world are usually implicit (as highlighted at the beginning of the chapter) and rely on the audience to understand the relationship between the propositions. However, it is important to be able to identify any additional premises on which the argument depends as making arguments explicit flags up bad reasoning and deductively invalid moves. Translating arguments into symbolic form has two uses; it provides a short-hand way of writing out arguments, but more importantly, it helps to clarify the structure of the argument. This separation of structure from content is helpful as it is easy to be side-tracked over whether the reasons or conclusions are true or not. Putting arguments into abstract forms by using symbols helps to avoid this confusion.

The next chapter will consider other aspects of assessing arguments. In particular, it will focus upon the truth of premises, observation and the credibility of sources.

Test Your Understanding

Learning Activity 3.5

State whether the following statements are true or false.

a) Deductive validity is when the reasons necessarily lead to the conclusion.

b) Verifying whether an argument is deductively valid is only one aspect of assessing whether an argument is a good one.

c) If it is clearly stated how the reasons lead to the conclusion then the argument's structure is explicit.

d) The symbol '∴' denotes a reason is being given.

e) 'If-then' arguments indicate a logical relationship between two things.

f) 'If p then q' means that whenever one is present then the other is also present.

g) 'Denying the antecedent' and 'affirming the consequent' indicate a good argument has been made.

●●▶

h) A syllogism is a special kind of argument that consists of two premises logically leading to a conclusion.

i) When using the circle system, if the position of the conclusion isn't clear from diagramming the reasons, then the argument is deductively invalid.

Chapter Review

What is meant by 'deductively valid'?

Deductively valid means that the reasons (premises) *necessarily* lead to the conclusion.

What is meant by the 'internal logic' of an argument?

Internal logic refers to the structure (or bare bones) of an argument and will determine whether the argument is deductively valid or not.

What is a proposition?

A *proposition* (in the context of critical thinking) is a statement that makes sense if placed on its own, such as 'Ed ran pretty fast' or 'They lost'. This is in contrast to part statements such as 'pretty fast' or 'lost', which are not propositions and do not make sense on their own.

What is a syllogism?

A syllogism is a special kind of deductively valid argument that consists of two premises logically leading to a conclusion.

What is meant by 'affirming the consequent' and 'denying the antecedent'?

These are forms of bad reasoning based on 'if-then' arguments. The 'consequent' refers to the 'then' part and the 'antecedent' refers to the 'if' part. If you *affirm the consequent* then you have mistakenly reasoned that because the 'then' part is true, the 'if' part must also be true. If you *deny the antecedent* then you have mistakenly reasoned that because the 'if' part is not true, then the 'then' part must also not be true. These are deductively invalid moves.

What is 'class logic'?

Class logic refers to deductive arguments that are based on classification systems and relationships between classes and with individuals.

All As are Bs	Some As are Bs	Some As are Bs
All Bs are Cs	All Bs are Cs	No Bs are Cs
∴ All As are Cs	∴ Some As are Cs	∴ Not all As are Cs
All As are Bs	If *p* then *q*	If *p* then *q*
No Bs are Cs	*p*	Not *q*
∴ No As are Cs	∴ *q*	∴ Not *p*
p or *q*	If *p* then *q*	If *p* then *q*
Not *p*	∴ If not *q* then not *p*	If *q* then *r*
∴ *q*		∴ If *p* then *r*

Table 3.1: Logical forms of deductively valid arguments.

All As are Bs	Some As are Bs	All As are Bs
All Cs are Bs	All Cs are As	No Cs are As
∴ All Cs are As	∴ Some Cs are Bs	∴ No Cs are Bs
If *p* then *q*	If *p* then *q*	If *p* then *q*
q	Not *p*	If *p* then *r*
∴ *p*	∴ Not *q*	∴ If *q* then *r*

Table 3.2: Logical forms of deductively invalid arguments.

Further Reading

Brown, A and Beyerstein, D (2003) *Critical Thinking: The Three Rs of College Life: Reading, Reasoning and wRiting.* Department of Philosophy: Langara College. (Can be found on www.langara.bc.ca/liberal-arts/philosophy/media/PDFs/criticalthinking.pdf. Accessed August 2009.) ★★★☆☆

This is a short but well-written introduction to critical thinking specifically aimed at undergraduate students. It contains a useful overview of deductive arguments and their logical forms.

Cryan, D, Shatil, S and Mayblin, B (2008) *Introducing Logic: A Graphic Guide.* Royston: Icon Books. ★★★★☆

The *Introducing* series attempts to present complex ideas in a primarily graphical format and *Introducing Logic* is no different. Using illustrations alongside a minimal amount of text, it can be a clear and motivating opening into what can be a very difficult and academic topic. If you find the logical forms in this chapter quite daunting, reading *Introducing Logic* is a good place to start.

Lau, J and Chan, J (2008) 'Argument Analysis' in *Critical Thinking Web*. (Can be found on
   www.philosophy.hku.hk/think/arg/arg.php. Accessed July 2009.) ★★★☆☆
This is a very useful online resource designed by the University of Hong Kong. It contains a good initial overview of critical thinking with a variety of exercises related to each aspect. This particular page contains accessible information and exercises on analysing arguments.

Reid, SP (2002) *How to Think: Building Your Mental Muscle*. London: Prentice-Hall. ★★☆☆☆
This book is primarily directed towards a business/management model of critical thinking and gives an impression of maudlin quality (that probably isn't helped by the cover and title). Nevertheless, there are some interesting and intelligent points raised and generally the layout is attractive with key statements highlighted in bold and embedded throughout the text.

Scriven, M (1976) *Reasoning*. London: McGraw-Hill. ★★★☆☆
In many ways, it is a shame that this book is no longer in print as it quite an engaging and informative critical thinking textbook. It is written in such a way that the student is forced to engage in critical reasoning and does so by providing questions and exercises but answering them in a way that suggests that there is still room for dialogue and argument. Scriven might be criticised for providing students with too much room for manoeuvre thus leading to a greater haziness of thought on their part, but my judgement is that he writes with a respect for the reader's intelligence that is comparable to the way that Socrates was able to elicit intelligent answers from those lacking in knowledge gained from formal education.

Answers to Learning Activities

Learning Activity 3.1

a) If Alice is a swimmer, and all swimmers like water, then what can we deduce about Alice? – *Alice must like water.*

b) All triathletes can swim, cycle and run. Oli can't swim. What can we deduce about Oli? – *Oli is not a triathlete.*

c) If Athavan is watching cricket, it must be a Saturday. It is a Saturday, so is there anything we can conclude about Athavan? – *We can't deduce a conclusion about Athavan's activities this Saturday. Just because Athavan only watches cricket on Saturday, it does not follow that every Saturday Athavan is watching cricket. To make this mistake is to affirm the consequent.*

d) Some athletes take illegal performance-enhancing substances. Caroline is an athlete, so is there any conclusion that follows? – *No conclusion can be reached as to whether Caroline takes illegal performance-enhancing substances as the statement is that only some, not all, athletes do so.*

e) All skate-boarders have good balance. Good balance requires good core stability. What can we deduce about skate-boarders? – *Skate-boarders have good core stability.*

f) Some footballers are goalkeepers. All goalkeepers are allowed to handle the ball. What else can we deduce about some footballers? – *Some footballers are allowed to handle the ball.*

Learning Activity 3.2

The additional reasons given are suggested answers. As long as the answer provides a logical connection between the reason and the conclusion, it should be acceptable. Conclusions (C) here are in italic, reasons (R) (AR = additional reason) are in bold.

a) *Usain won the 100m sprint* (C) because **he had a fast stride frequency and a long stride length** (R). (AR) **Success in the 100m sprint is dependent on stride frequency and stride length.**

b) *Six Australasian Crusader players are to be deported* (C) due to **visa irregularities** (R). (AR) **If a person does not have a correct visa then they will be deported.**

c) **Too many unforced errors** (R) *led to a straight sets loss for Venus in the Toronto Cup* (C). (AR) **Unforced errors will give the opponent easy points, which makes it much more difficult to win games and therefore sets.**

d) **Tamsyn showed she was knowledgeable, hard-working and could react quickly to orders** (R). Therefore *she was selected as part of the team for the Fastnet race* (C). (AR) **Competing in the Fastnet race requires people who demonstrate attributes such as good knowledge, diligence and reacting quickly to orders.**

e) *Smith pleaded for more money to be given to GB gymnastics* (C) in order **to improve results** (R). (AR) **Money will contribute to success in GB gymnastics.**

f) *The Austrian men's doubles are the latest to withdraw from the Badminton World Championships in India* (C) **amid security fears** (R). (AR) **Players will withdraw from competitions if they believe that their security is at risk.**

Learning Activity 3.3

a) All As are Bs. (All gymnasts are supple)
   All Bs are Cs. (All those who are supple have a wide range of movement)
   ∴ All As are Cs. (All gymnasts have a wide range of movement)

b) No As are Bs. (No human has run faster than 30mph)
   All Cs are As. (All Olympic champions are human)
   ∴ No Cs are Bs. (No Olympic champion has run faster than 30mph)

c) If *p* then *q*. (If a competitor finishes in the top three then he will automatically qualify for the final)
   p. (Tom finished second)
   ∴ *q*. (Tom will automatically qualify for the final)

d) All As are Bs. (All NBA players are men)
   Some Cs are As. (Some basketball players are NBA players)
   ∴ Some Cs are Bs. (Some basketball players are men)

e) If p then q. (If a coronary artery becomes blocked it will cause a heart attack)
Not q. (There has been no heart attack)
∴ not p. (A coronary artery isn't blocked)

f) p or q. (The 2011 Asian Games will be hosted by either Qatar or Australia)
Not p. (Qatar has pulled out)
∴ q. (The 2011 Asian Games will be hosted by Australia)

Learning Activity 3.4

a) Karen is a surfer. All surfers are able to swim. Therefore, Karen is able to swim.
This argument is *deductively valid* (Figure 3.19).

b) The javelin is a field event. Athletics comprises track and field events. Therefore, the javelin is part of athletics.
This argument is *deductively valid* (Figure 3.20).

c) All badminton players have quick reaction speeds. All slip fielders have quick reaction speeds. Therefore, all badminton players are slip fielders.
This argument is *deductively invalid* as it isn't clear as to what class(es) the category of slip fielder belongs (Figure 3.21).

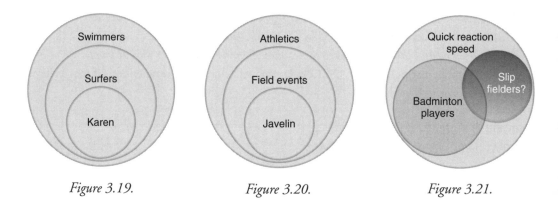

Figure 3.19.   Figure 3.20.   Figure 3.21.

d) Acrophobics do not like heights. Those that do not like heights will not go base-jumping. Therefore, acrophobics will not go base-jumping.
This argument is *deductively valid* (Figure 3.22).

e) Testing VO$_2$ max is a way of assessing physical fitness. Physical fitness can also be tested via a 20m shuttle run. Therefore, a 20m shuttle run is a way of testing VO$_2$ max.
The conclusion is not determined by the premises so the argument is *deductively invalid* (Figure 3.23).

f) Sport is a form of exercise. Exercise is a leisure pursuit. Therefore, sport is a leisure pursuit.
This argument is *deductively valid* (Figure 3.24).

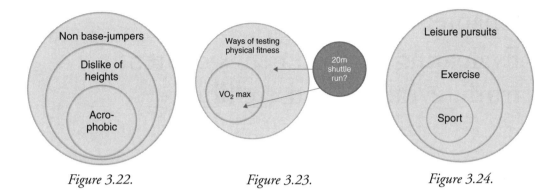

Figure 3.22.   Figure 3.23.   Figure 3.24.

Learning Activity 3.5

a) Deductive validity is when the reasons necessarily lead to the conclusion. – *TRUE.*

b) Verifying whether an argument is deductively valid is only one aspect of assessing whether an argument is a good one. – *TRUE (It is possible for the argument to be deductively valid and yet the reasons to be untrue, which would make the argument a bad one).*

c) If it is clearly stated how the reasons lead to the conclusion then the argument's structure is explicit. – *TRUE.*

d) The symbol '∴' denotes a reason is being given. – *FALSE (∴ stands for 'therefore' and indicates a conclusion is being given).*

e) 'If-then' arguments indicate a logical relationship between two things. – *TRUE.*

f) 'If *p* then *q*' means that whenever one is present then the other is also present. – *FALSE (Unless stated otherwise, this only works in one direction; that is, 'if q' does not mean 'then p').*

g) 'Denying the antecedent' and 'affirming the consequent' indicate a good argument has been made. – *FALSE (These are the technical names for particular types of bad reasoning).*

h) A syllogism is a special kind of argument that consists of two premises logically leading to a conclusion. – *TRUE.*

i) When using the circle system, if the position of the conclusion isn't clear from diagramming the reasons, then the argument is deductively invalid. – *TRUE.*

Chapter 4
Evaluating an argument's content: truth, evidence and credibility

Learning Objectives

This chapter will help you:

- evaluate the content of arguments;
- evaluate evidence given in arguments;
- assess the credibility of sources.

Look at the following argument and decide whether it seems a reasonable one:

a) Only those countries that won a medal in the last Olympic Games will be allowed to compete in the next Olympic Games.
b) China didn't win any medals in the last Olympic Games.
c) Therefore, China will not be allowed to compete in the next Olympic Games.

Hopefully, you noticed that this argument is flawed. If you have read the last chapter, you may accept that it is a good argument in terms of its logical structure, in that it is deductively valid, but you would still want to reject it due to its content. So whilst the previous chapter focused upon what makes an argument a good one from a structural point of view, this chapter will concentrate on the other side in evaluating arguments: the *content*.

The example given above contains a valid conclusion that logically follows from the reasons, so it is an argument, but the problem is that the reasons that are given are untrue. The concept of truth is a problematic one that philosophers have spent millennia debating. So, although this chapter will briefly touch upon the nature of truth, it will subsequently settle on the presumption that good arguments rest upon good evidence and good evidence can be constituted in many forms.

The 'truth' is out there . . .

The concept of truth is a very tricky one and it's easy to play the role of a sceptic. Even the most reasonable of assumptions, for instance that the sun will rise tomorrow, or that water will flow downwards rather than upwards when I run the shower after a game, have been subject to some very persuasive criticism (Figure 4.1).

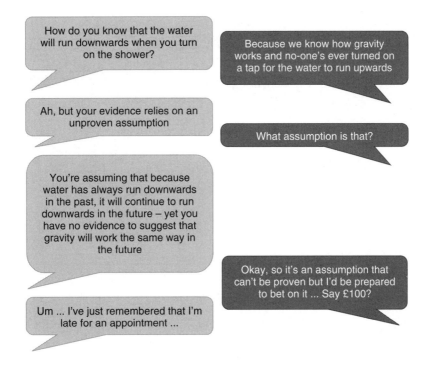

Figure 4.1.

The only statements that can be said to be absolutely true are called *analytic* statements: that is, they are true by definition. So for instance, statements such as 'Football is Fußball' or 'a metatarsal fracture is a broken foot' are true without recourse to any evidence other than the meaning of those terms. One criticism in preserving the concept of truth solely to analytic statements is that they are simply tautological and are devoid of content. In effect, you are merely saying 'Football is Football' and 'a broken foot is a broken foot'. That is not to say definition of terms is unimportant for it can help to clarify meaning and highlight where misunderstandings have taken place. It also allows for greater discussion of more contested concepts where there is no agreed definition. The concept of 'sport' itself is one of these contested terms, which, although it can provide an amusing topic for pub conversations, has implications on policy and practice. For instance, should a funding bid presented to a sports body on behalf of a tiddlywinks club be given the same consideration as a funding bid from a netball club? It may all depend on whether tiddlywinks is classified as a sport or not. See Figure 4.2 for a further example of analytic and synthetic statements.

Ultimately many disagreements come down to the meaning of key terms. When evaluating and constructing arguments, it is important to try to clarify what is meant by particular contested concepts and even if they remain ethereal then simply noting that there is some ambiguity will help in coming to a resolution.

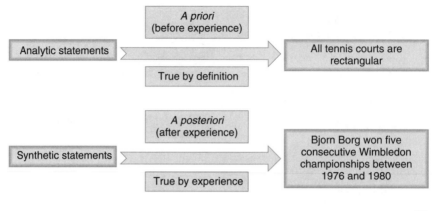

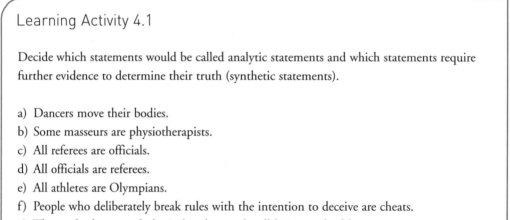

Figure 4.2.

Learning Activity 4.1

Decide which statements would be called analytic statements and which statements require further evidence to determine their truth (synthetic statements).

a) Dancers move their bodies.
b) Some masseurs are physiotherapists.
c) All referees are officials.
d) All officials are referees.
e) All athletes are Olympians.
f) People who deliberately break rules with the intention to deceive are cheats.
g) Those who have good physical and mental well-being are healthy.
h) Rally drivers race cars.

Evidence

One of the benefits of evaluating the truth of claims that are dependent on the definition of key terms or concepts (analytic statements) is that it doesn't require the testing of external evidence. It can be done in the comfort of one's armchair so to speak. However, when it comes to evaluating arguments, claims that are dependent on verifying some external experience (synthetic statements) are those that we are generally faced with. For instance, if you are in charge of a marketing department that needs to get ahead of your competitors and are told that Budapest has been awarded the Olympics over Stockholm, then in order to plan an effective marketing strategy for your company, you need to decide whether the claim is true or not. If the claim turns out to be false and you have already committed much of your budget on the presumption that it was true, then you might soon find yourself out of a job.

Learning Activity 4.2

Decide what evidence would be required for you to accept the following claims to be true.

a) Beth is playing squash.
b) Oxford have won 12 of the last 14 boat races.
c) The action of knee flexion produced by the hamstrings is an example of a third-class lever.
d) Nottingham Forest FC are playing Reading FC next weekend.
e) Polo originated from China over 2,000 years ago.
f) Wales will win the 4 × 400m men's relay in the next Commonwealth Games.
g) Salibandyliiga is the professional floorball league of Finland.
h) Surf lifesaving is a sport.

Observation

One way of judging whether a reason or claim is a good one is whether it has been observed to have occurred or not. We generally base judgements about the world on information gained through our own senses and if this can be corroborated with the observation of others then it is strengthened further. Nevertheless, however reliable we believe our observations to be, there are still several things that need to be taken into account.

Distinguishing observation from speculation

Barristers in a court of law will often attempt to distinguish between a witness providing a theory about what happened and their actual observation. The following example illustrates this. Imagine a case where Sam is walking home from work and he sees a group of Dundee supporters emerging from the pub. They are in high spirits and when Sam asks them what the score was, they reply '2–0'. Later that evening, Sam tells his friends that Dundee won 2–0. Sam's conclusion that Dundee had won may be a reasonable one, for we associate a team's winning with high spirits amongst that team's players and supporters, but in fact Dundee had lost 2–0. However, it wasn't an important match and the result was eclipsed by one of the supporters winning a significant amount of money on the lottery and treating his friends to a night out. Had Sam's friends asked him whether he had any evidence that Dundee had won or whether he had simply deduced a (false) conclusion from other evidence, he would have admitted that it was just a theory (Figure 4.3).

It is important therefore to assess whether something has actually been observed or whether a conclusion has been deduced about some other observation that was made.

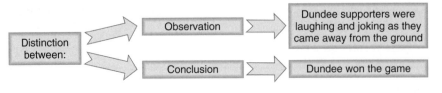

Figure 4.3.

Observation conditions

Although relying on observation is an important way to decide whether a statement is true or not, even first-person observation can be fallible. If conditions are poor, for instance if it is dark and foggy and you had forgotten to put on your glasses, then relying on your observation is more problematic than if it was a bright day and your sight was excellent. Another factor that needs to be taken into account is the difference in time between an observation and recalling it as memories become blurred and affected by other events. Making a judgement about conditions for observation is an important consideration especially when weighing up conflicting information.

Bias and attention

Bias and attention also need to be taken into account when assessing observation statements. It's not uncommon to find that when your attention is drawn towards something, you see more instances of it. If we buy a new car, for instance, we seem to suddenly notice many other similar cars on the road. One of the criticisms of sports trials is that the coaches tend to pick players that they already know and therefore it is difficult for a new player to get selected. One reason for this could be that a coach's attention is already drawn to those players they're already aware of whilst other players are beyond their scope of attention. So unless a new player showcases some exceptional skill to get herself noticed, a known player of similar ability will often be selected above her.

Technology

Many scientific observations rely on technology: astronomers will use telescopes, biologists will use microscopes and climate scientists will use computer simulations. Despite the perennial fears that introducing a particular technology will be detrimental to a sport, the use of technology in order to make those decisions that are difficult by relying on the human senses alone is becoming increasingly common. However, this is not to say that such technology is infallible. For instance, Hawkeye in cricket has been criticised for giving the impression, particularly to the general public, that it is 100 per cent accurate in determining whether the ball would have hit the stumps or not. The computer program behind the graphics is only able to produce a prediction of events based on the information that it is given. This information may be inaccurate or incomplete. Similarly, the use of touchpads in swimming competitions has been criticised for the technology registering a touch when it hasn't occurred and vice versa. So, although technology can be a helpful aid in determining the truth of a statement, it should always be remembered that it isn't definitive and can give unreliable data.

Reports

Second-hand observation can come in a variety of forms. Someone else might directly report what they observed or what someone else told them had been observed. Reports can be written evidence, in forms such as official documents or papers that have been peer reviewed, diaries or weblogs, newspaper articles, raw data from experiments, surveys or censuses.

Hearsay

Hearsay is generally the least credible type of source as it inherently magnifies all the problems highlighted with observation since it involves more than one person. This is why hearsay is not admitted in court evidence. Everyone familiar with the game 'Chinese Whispers' or 'Whisper Down the Lane' will recognise that part of the amusement stems from seeing how a message has become mistranslated or distorted as it is passed from person to person. Sometimes this distortion is a deliberate embellishment, other times it can simply be misheard or badly recalled. As this is a reflection of real life, statements based on the memory of someone who is recalling someone else's memory, and so on, can be a very poor source for the truth even when there is no intention to mislead.

Diaries and weblogs

The important distinction between diaries and weblogs is that the latter is likely to be accessible on the internet at the time of writing, whereas diaries are generally published years after they are written. This difference may, though does not necessarily, mean that diaries are less self-censored than weblogs, although it depends on the purpose behind them. They are both useful sources of information in gleaning aspects of motivation and personality but as there is little accountability to ensure that information is accurately reported, the evidence may not be as rigorously investigated as in other sources. Nevertheless, there are some very highly respected weblogs written by experts that attempt to provide accurate and reliable information and shy away from simply expressing subjective opinion. This is particularly the case for those people employed to write a blog in a professional capacity. The key in assessing this information is to judge the credibility of the person writing it (something that is discussed later) and question what type of weblog it is, whether in the form of a traditional diary that shares an individual's daily life and their feelings about it, or whether it is attempting to provide a porthole of information on a specific subject.

Official documents

Officially written and published documents and reports, such as government papers, policy documents, transcriptions of hearings or events and data from censuses, are often considered to be the most reliable and credible type of evidence. As the authors are writing the documents in an official capacity, the procedures behind their publication are much more rigorous than for an individual writing a diary in a personal capacity. However, all governments and official bodies are likely to promote their own agenda and values and therefore may present certain information and statistical evidence in a particular light to suit their aims. This is presumption behind the famous phrase: 'There are three types of falsehoods; lies, damned lies, and statistics.'

Statistics

Raw data from experiments, surveys and censuses can be analysed to indicate correlation between different variables, norms and anomalies. But this analysis is only as good as the original data. If a study is carried out that asks people about their participation in sport but there are only ten participants and they are questioned after a training night at a netball centre, then the conclusions that follow from the data analysis would be very different had the participants come from a care home for the elderly (see Chapter 5 for more information on sample size).

Reliability of research

The reliability of research is whether the results can be equally applied to a wider population. National surveys or censuses can provide the most reliable sources of information as they theoretically cover every member of the population and there is a legal obligation to complete the census form. However, despite this obligation, some decline to respond, and it may be that those that do not respond have other commonalities that would also affect the overall census results had they been taken into account.

Validity of research

The other strand of good evidence in research is its validity. The term 'validity', in this sense, is slightly different to the one we used when discussing valid arguments. For research to be valid, it needs to focus on or measure what it intends and not inadvertently something else. An example here could be a test to measure the effectiveness of imagery techniques before carrying out a goal-kicking task. Let us say that the research participant is asked to kick at goal ten times and her successful score is measured. She is then asked to imagine herself kicking a goal successfully and is then tested for another ten attempts. If these last ten kicks are more successful than the first ten it could be concluded that imagery was effective in her performance. However, it could be just as likely that imagery had nothing to do with the greater success in her later kicks, rather it could be due to the practice of having the first ten kicks, having become more relaxed with the environment, a sudden change in wind conditions, or many other variables. As such, this research would be said to lack validity because it might not be measuring the very thing that it aims to measure (i.e. the effect of imagery on performance).

Historical documents

Historical documents, whether personal diaries or official records, should be regarded in the same light as has already been outlined above, depending on the type of document. However, historical documents need to be viewed in the context in which they were written. So documents that were written prior to the advent of particular technologies, such as fast transport systems, copying machines and developments in scientific knowledge, need to be viewed as such. Again, this reiterates issues of reliability and validity in collecting data. Furthermore, historical documents will provide a picture or conception of the world that is contained within a larger social context. One only has to read historical accounts of the altruistic colonization of 'primitive peoples' in documents written as recently as the early twentieth century to see how our depictions and interpretation of events change with time. Again, discretion should be used in determining how useful historical documentation and records can be in providing evidence for a claim.

Learning Activity 4.3

State the type of evidence provided in each example and comment on its advantages and drawbacks.

a) 'Britain's top sports lawyer has warned Alex Ferguson that Alan Wiley [a Premiership referee] would be justified in suing him – to stop his "bullying"' (Facey, 2009).
b) As you leave the court chatting to your opposition about the game, you think you spot one of the national selectors walking away. By the time you finish your current conversation and look again, you are unable to see her.
c) 'Last Sunday's *New York Times* included a very interesting essay by Alice Dreger [reprinted at this link] that accuses sport philosophers of lagging behind sport scientists. She concludes that we need to reach consensus on what sport is really all about before we can adequately address such issues as steroid use and sex determination' (Reid, 2009).
d) 'The Prime Minister announced the Olympic International Inspiration programme . . . during his visit to India in January 2008. This pilot programme, which runs until 2010, involves five countries, one from each of the Olympic regions: Brazil, Zambia, Palau, Azerbaijan and India and represents a £9 million investment' (Department of Culture, Media and Sport Annual Report, 2008).
e) '49,700 adults (age 16 and over) participated in archery at least once in the last four weeks. This represents 0.12% of the adult population' (Archery Factsheet, 2008).

Assessing the credibility of sources

Some of the issues concerning the credibility of others have already been touched upon but there are other aspects that need to be considered. Ennis (1996) provides eight criteria for assessing how much weight should be given to a particular source.

Background experience and knowledge

If I started advising marathon runners on training programmes and race tactics then I would be quite concerned if anyone actually followed my advice since I know absolutely nothing about long-distance running, except that Kenya seems to produce quite a few successful athletes in this discipline. As I have no background experience in long-distance or marathon running and I have no technical knowledge about what is the best way to prepare for one, then my credibility is greatly diminished. If, however, a player were to ask my advice on general fitness for rugby then my background experience and knowledge would give my words much more credibility. When assessing evidence, ask the question, 'Do they have any knowledge or experience of the issue?' If you discover that this person has no personal experience or knowledge on the issue then judge their credibility accordingly.

Lack of apparent conflict of interest

I previously used the example of a selector who already knew several of the players and is likely therefore to be biased towards them. If this selector was already a coach of these players in another capacity (let's say that he was a club coach and a regional selector) then arguably he would have a conflict of interest between wanting his players to be selected and having the power to select them over others. In this case, the coach's conflict of interest could be down to wanting to provide opportunity to his players, wanting recognition for his club, or because he didn't want to face the questioning by known parents. Sometimes a conflict of interest could be a financial gain. If the coach's contract at his club was renewed on the basis of how many players had been selected for the regional team then the coach would be under pressure to ensure that his own players were selected. Conflicts of interest don't necessarily mean that the source is corrupt, merely that they may be pressured to act in a particular way for reasons other than those that they give. The question that needs to be considered is, 'Do they have anything to gain from promoting their view?' If the answer is no, then the source's credibility is enhanced.

Agreement with others equally qualified

We would generally accept that the more people who are in agreement on a particular issue (and also satisfy the other criteria), the more credible the evidence. If two sports therapists, for example, independently assessed the nature of a player's injury and came to the same conclusion, then we would be more willing to accept that conclusion. This is why second (or third) opinions are called upon, to corroborate or disconfirm the first opinion. However, this is not to say that majority opinion is always the right one. There are many instances of expert agreement later being discredited, for example the consensus amongst natural philosophers (what we would now call scientists) that the heart was the seat of the soul and intelligence. This conception of the function of the heart was widely accepted until the late sixteenth century. Another similarly discredited but popularly held claim was the view held in the nineteenth and early twentieth century that women's bodies were too weak and feeble to withstand the demands of participation in sport. Nevertheless, if the question is asked, 'Is there agreement amongst experts on this?', an answer in the affirmative generally strengthens a source's credibility.

Reputation

The saying, 'you never get a second chance to make a first impression' highlights the degree to which people get judged on their past behaviour. Just as a player gets selected or dropped on her past performance, sources that have a reputation for being poor or false will be considered less credible than those that have a history of being accurate and trustworthy. In order to assess credibility, the question should be asked, 'Do they have a precedent of being reliable or unreliable?'

Known risk to reputation

The more risk of harm to a source's reputation, the less likely they are to make a bold claim. This means that a source is likely to err on the side of caution if their reputation would be damaged if that claim turned out not to be true. So for example, if a well-respected sport scientist endorsed a training aid on the grounds that it improved an individual's reaction time, and it turned out that there was no evidence supporting this claim, it would likely harm the reputation of the sport scientist. Arguably, if all other criteria for good credibility are satisfied and the sports scientist is prepared to make such a claim, then the source's credibility is enhanced. The question that needs to be asked is, 'What effect would it have on the source's reputation if their claim was shown to be false?'

Established procedures

If there are already procedures in place for determining a particular outcome, and if those procedures have been followed, credibility is strengthened. This is due to the fact that procedures generally arise from a considered review of the most effective course of action to ensure that a particular outcome is realised. For example, the procedures in place to appoint a youth coach may involve criminal record checks, the collection of references, formal interviews and seeing evidence of coaching qualifications. These procedures are in place to ensure that it is less likely for the children and young people to be put at risk if a coach is hired. So having followed such procedures, claims as to the trustworthiness of the coach are given greater credibility. The question to be asked is, 'Have established procedures been followed that would enhance or weaken the power of the claim?'

Ability to give reasons

If someone is able to back up their claim by providing further evidence and reasons to support it, then it holds more weight in being true. When analysing a golf swing for example, an instructor might claim that it is the player's head movement that is causing them problems. They could call upon video evidence to support this claim, hold the player's head still while they swing to kinaesthetically illustrate the difference in movement or show biomechanically how a movement of the head would affect other aspects of the body and ultimately the swing. There may be times whereby someone is unable to give further reasons to support their claim, especially if this relies upon observations for example. If an official rules a player to have stepped outside the field of play and there was no further evidence to support or refute the claim, then it would be futile to ask for the official to provide further reasons. All she would be able to say would be, 'I just saw it.' Here, you need to use your judgement in deciding whether it is reasonable to ask for more evidence. The important question here is, 'Can the source provide any additional reasons or evidence to support their claim?'

Careful habits

This criterion is related to the one of reputation. If a source has a reputation for having careful or careless habits this can be used as a way of assessing credibility. For example, if the individual who is responsible for ensuring that all pre-match preparations run smoothly and is known for his thoroughness and reliability claims that another individual who has a habit of being careless and lazy is responsible for the water bottles being empty, then it is likely that his claim is credible. The question to be asked is, 'Are they known for their careful habits?' If the answer is yes, then any claim that went against this view would be weakened.

Overview of credibility criteria

An overview of the credibility criteria discussed in the previous section is given in Figure 4.4.

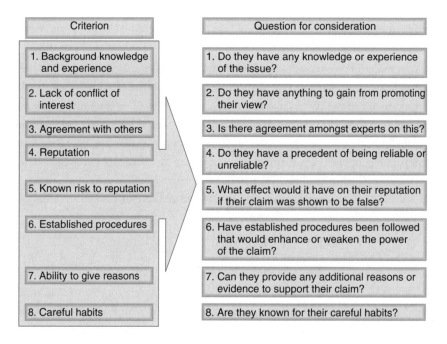

Criterion	Question for consideration
1. Background knowledge and experience	1. Do they have any knowledge or experience of the issue?
2. Lack of conflict of interest	2. Do they have anything to gain from promoting their view?
3. Agreement with others	3. Is there agreement amongst experts on this?
4. Reputation	4. Do they have a precedent of being reliable or unreliable?
5. Known risk to reputation	5. What effect would it have on their reputation if their claim was shown to be false?
6. Established procedures	6. Have established procedures been followed that would enhance or weaken the power of the claim?
7. Ability to give reasons	7. Can they provide any additional reasons or evidence to support their claim?
8. Careful habits	8. Are they known for their careful habits?

Figure 4.4.

Learning Activity 4.4

Using the criteria and the associated questions, assess the credibility of the claim made in the following cases.

a) 'We're going to have to work considerably on our fitness over the next few weeks. We are struggling to get round the park for the last quarter of the match at the moment and other teams are taking advantage of that fact,' said Steve Penfold, Leeds head coach and senior lecturer in sports performance at Loughborough University.

b) Harry Winch, who has recently started supporting the local village team, Hethersett, said to his friend, 'You know that old guy with the dog who always turns up to watch the men play on a Saturday afternoon? Well he told me that he'd heard that the board aren't happy with the level of coaching the players are getting at the moment. They're trying to get rid of the head coach and replace him with this guy from up country.'

c) It has been confirmed that Wiles and Keating, the company that recently launched the new sports drink 'Powershot', will be the club's main sponsor for the next season. Club captain and former international player, Anna-Marie Jones, has endorsed the new product saying, 'Powershot definitely gives players a performance edge that allows them to focus harder for longer. I wish the product had been around when I was competing.'

d) An independent right-wing political blog has claimed that taxes will rise to cover the exorbitant costs of hosting the Olympics. It stated: 'Secret sources have admitted that the original estimates for hosting the Olympics were completely off target. The gaping black hole left in the finances will have to be covered by an increase in public taxes.'

e) A coach for an under 15s rugby team confides in his regional manager that he suspects one of his players is suffering abuse at home. He then informs the child welfare manager and documents his concerns and the reasons he has for them, and ensures the document is kept confidential at all times.

This chapter has provided an overview of the ways in which arguments can be evaluated on the truth or reasonableness of their premises. It has considered what sorts of things constitute good evidence and how to judge whether a source is credible or not. The following chapter will continue to assess the content of arguments, in particular by looking at the assumptions on which many arguments are based.

Test Your Understanding

Learning Activity 4.5

State whether the following statements are true or false.

a) An argument is good if the reasons given for the conclusion are true.
b) Synthetic statements are those that are true by definition whilst analytic statements rest upon observation from experience.
c) It is easy to verify the truth of a claim.
d) When assessing arguments it is important to highlight concepts or terms that might be contested.
e) Claims that are based on hearsay will always be false.

●●●▶

f) Statistics provide conclusive evidence.

g) If a source's reputation is likely to be damaged if their claim is disproved then their credibility is enhanced.

h) If someone has a conflict of interests then their credibility as a source will be reduced.

Chapter Review

What constitutes 'truth'?

Truth is a difficult concept to identify but in the area of critical thinking it is best to consider it as states of affairs or propositions about the world that are justified by recourse to good evidence and reasoning.

What is the difference between analytic and synthetic statements?

An *analytic statement* is one that can be verified simply by understanding the meaning of the concepts contained within it (e.g. 'A goal is scored when the ball crosses the line'). A *synthetic statement* is one that is verified by considering evidence from the external world (e.g. 'Max scored a goal').

What is evidence?

Evidence is information that justifies a particular claim. This can be gained from a variety of sources, for example through direct observation, reports, data collected from technological innovations, publications etc.

What is meant by statistical reliability and validity?

Statistical *reliability* means the data can be generalised to a wider population. Statistical *validity* means that the data is measuring what is intended to be measured and not alternative phenomena.

What is the credibility of a source?

Credibility refers to the reliability of the information that is being given in support of a claim. As humans, we have a variety of interests and biases that may affect the reliability of our claims or observations. In assessing credibility, consideration needs to be taken to weigh up these fallibilities.

Further Reading

Bowell, T and Kemp, G (2005) *Critical Thinking: A Concise Guide* (second edition). London: Routledge. ★★★★☆

The scope of critical thinking is underlined when a book containing over 300 large pages claims to be a 'concise guide'. Nevertheless, Bowell and Kemp do justice to this claim by covering all the relevant aspects of critical thinking but in a sufficiently detailed and accessible way. The final chapter on the concepts of truth and knowledge is helpful in highlighting to students that the all too familiar relativistic response to a debate ('that may be true for you but not for me . . .') is no response at all.

Phelen, P and Reynolds, P (1996) *Argument and Evidence: A Critical Analysis for the Social Sciences.* London: Routledge. ★★★☆☆

Although some of the examples given are slightly dated and often from the political arena, this book not only covers the range of issues concerned with evaluating arguments but also focuses upon interpreting data collected from experiments and surveys. The end of chapter reviews are particularly useful and succinct as are the chapters dealing with definitional problems, presenting and summarising data as evidence and determining probability.

Van den Brink-Budgen, R (2000) *Critical Thinking for Students* (third edition). Oxford: Howtobooks. ★☆☆☆☆

This book is designed primarily for pre-undergraduate-level students so although it covers much of the relevant material concerning argument construction and evaluation, it does so in significantly less depth than the general undergraduate-level text. This may mean that it is much less daunting than the Ennis (1996) book, for example, but there are arguably many other better introductory texts than this one.

Answers to Learning Activities

Learning Activity 4.1

A good way of deciding whether a statement is analytic or not is to try to imagine a world whereby the statement is false, so for instance, it is possible to imagine a world whereby no officials are referees (referees in this world wouldn't exist – all officials would be time keepers or organisers for instance) but it is not possible to imagine a world where none of the referees are officials. The term 'referee' by definition has to entail being an official.

a) Dancers move their bodies. – *Analytic: It is impossible to conceive of a dancer that doesn't move his body.*

b) Some masseurs are physiotherapists. – *Synthetic: A masseur by definition does not have to be a physiotherapist.*

c) All referees are officials. – *Analytic: Being a referee means that one is also an official.*

d) All officials are referees. – *Synthetic: There may be officials who are not referees.*

e) All athletes are Olympians. – *Synthetic: The definition of athlete does not entail being an Olympian.*

f) People who deliberately break rules with the intention to deceive are cheats. – *Analytic: This may be contested to an extent since the term 'cheat' has some moral force behind it, i.e. that it is unjustified, but it is nevertheless a reasonable definition of the term.*

g) Those who have good physical and mental well-being are healthy. – *Analytic: Being healthy, by definition, requires good physical and mental well-being.*

h) Rally drivers race cars. – *Analytic: It is impossible to conceive of a rally driver who doesn't race cars.*

Learning Activity 4.2

There are no absolute answers to the questions since what constitutes evidence relies to a great extent upon judgement. However, as the chapter outlines, there are different types of evidence depending on what is required for acceptance and so suggestions to answers are provided.

a) Beth is playing squash. – *This may be accepted on the basis of direct observation, indirect observation (reported observation), or by what Beth herself had said she'd be doing.*

b) Oxford have won 12 of the last 14 boat races. – *This could be verified by looking at official records of events or past newspaper articles.*

c) The action of knee flexion produced by the hamstrings is an example of a third-class lever. – *This is an analytical statement that is true by definition.*

d) Nottingham Forest FC are playing Reading FC next weekend. – *Official league fixtures would constitute reasonable evidence although a statement from a credible and trustworthy source could be equally acceptable.*

e) Polo originated from China over 2,000 years ago. – *These types of historical statements are much more difficult to verify as they depend on interpretation of other historical documents which may or may not be whole and accurate records of events.*

f) Wales will win the 4 × 400m men's relay in next year's Commonwealth Games. – *This statement cannot be verified as it is a prediction of future events, which may or may not be true at a later time. However, reasonable predictions about the future can be made from evidence from similar events in the past.*

g) Salibandyliiga is the professional floorball league of Finland. – *This is part analytic statement – that Salibandyliiga is translated as 'floorball league' in Finnish – but also can be verified by direct observation or official documents.*

h) Surf lifesaving is a sport. – *Accepting this statement as true is dependent on the definition of contested concepts, e.g. 'sport', and so it is a matter of judgement rather than evidence.*

Learning Activity 4.3

a) 'Britain's top sports lawyer has warned Alex Ferguson that Alan Wiley would be justified in suing him – to stop his "bullying"' (Facey, 2009). – *This is a newspaper article that reports a claim by another person. Since the information is from a secondary source (the* Sun *newspaper) it may suffer from the problems of hearsay, in that a statement is misreported or taken out of context. Additionally, the* Sun *newspaper, due to its style of reporting and intended audience and reading age, is regarded by some to be a less credible source than other news outlets. Nevertheless, it still has to maintain certain standards in reporting (or suffer libel claims) and has to be approved by the editor. Although the quoted source is named later in the article, no further evidence is given as to why this person is considered by the* Sun *as 'Britain's top sports lawyer'.*

b) As you leave the court chatting to your opposition about the game, you think you spot one of the national selectors walking away. By the time you finish your current conversation and look again, you are unable to see her. – *This is a direct observation. However, the conditions for this observation need to be taken into account. At the time of the observation, your attention was directed elsewhere (to the conversation with your opponent). The observed person was walking away so presumably you were only able to see them from behind and not their face. The observation was fleeting and could not be verified by later observation. Although you (presumably) have good eyesight, the circumstances mean that you would be likely to want to find other evidence to support the original claim.*

c) 'Last Sunday's *New York Times* included a very interesting essay by Alice Dreger [reprinted at this link] that accuses sport philosophers of lagging behind sport scientists. She concludes that we need to reach consensus on what sport is really all about before we can adequately address such issues as steroid use and sex determination' (Reid, 2009). – *As this is from an independent blog it could suffer from a lack of accuracy in the information it reports since it lacks real accountability. It summarises a claim made by a secondary source so there may be some misrepresentation of the views given in the original source. However, the blog is a collaborative one written by named academic experts who arguably would not wish to write anything that might damage their reputation. Additionally, a link to the original article is provided that would allow cross-checking to take place.*

d) 'The Prime Minister announced the Olympic International Inspiration programme . . . during his visit to India in January 2008. This pilot programme, which runs until 2010, involves five countries, one from each of the Olympic regions: Brazil, Zambia, Palau, Azerbaijan and India and represents a £9 million investment' (Department of Culture, Media and Sport Annual Report, 2008). – *Although this document can be found online, it is an official government paper that has been through a rigorous process to ensure that the information it provides is accurate. It is likely that since it is a political document, the information contained within it will be presented to show the government in the best possible light. For instance, there is some slightly ambiguous language, i.e. 'represents' £9 million (which indicates that someone has equated the project to be worth £9 million, rather than actually giving £9 million).*

e) '49,700 adults (age 16 and over) participated in archery at least once in the last four weeks. This represents 0.12% of the adult population' (Archery Factsheet, 2008). – *Again, this is a government-funded document and therefore the information contained within it would have been compiled by those in an official capacity with some accountability for accurate reporting. Although information given later in the document does provide some basic information on methodology and statistical analysis, as the information comes from a survey but has been generalised out across the population as a whole it may suffer from errors in reliability and validity.*

Learning Activity 4.4

The suggested answers ought to be used merely as a guide to assessing credibility and are not definitive. This is because the examples are limited in depth and there is a lot of information that is missing or unknown. More detailed examples and case studies can be found in a later chapter.

a) 'We're going to have to work considerably on our fitness over the next few weeks. We are struggling to get round the park for the last quarter of the match at the moment and other teams are taking advantage of that fact,' said Steve Penfold, Leeds head coach and senior lecturer in sports performance at Loughborough University.

- *Background knowledge and experience*: Excellent.
- *Lack of apparent conflict of interest*: Good.
- *Agreement with others*: Unknown.
- *Reputation*: Good (on the basis of position of head coach and other employment).
- *Risk to reputation*: Reasonably high (if the coach was unable to accurately identify areas for improvement then he may lose his contract).
- *Established procedures*: Unknown (although the claim may be supported by data from fitness tests and other analysis).
- *Ability to give reasons*: Fair (alluded to poorer performance in latter quarter of the match that may indicate lack of fitness).
- *Careful habits*: Unknown.
- *Overall*: **credibility for claim is good.**

b) Harry Winch, who has recently started supporting the local village team, Hethersett, said to his friend, 'You know that old guy with the dog who always turns up to watch the men play on a Saturday afternoon? Well he told me that he'd heard that the board aren't happy with the level of coaching the players are getting at the moment. They're trying to get rid of the head coach and replace him with this guy from up country.'

- *Background knowledge and experience*: Fairly poor (as Harry is stated to be a recent supporter of the team. The claim is also hearsay. It is unknown who the 'old guy with the dog' is and whether he has any background knowledge or experience. It could be argued that if the man with the dog was also a member of the board, or had direct links with the board, then he would have been described as such, e.g. 'That guy with the dog, who's called . . . and is on the board of directors . . .').
- *Lack of apparent conflict of interest*: Good (though additional information may uncover that the source has a vested interest or personal reason to oust the head coach).
- *Agreement with others*: Poor (there is no evidence to suggest that others agree with the claim made, since it is based on a single piece of hearsay).
- *Reputation*: Unknown.
- *Risk to reputation*: Low (since the claim was said to his friend, it is unlikely that there will be repercussions to Harry's reputation if it turns out to be false).
- *Established procedures*: None.
- *Ability to give reasons*: Poor (no reasons are given).

- *Careful habits*: Unknown.
- *Overall*: *credibility for claim is low.*

c) It has been confirmed that Wiles and Keating, the company that recently launched the new sports drink 'Powershot', will be the club's main sponsor for the next season. Club captain and former international player, Anna-Marie Jones, has endorsed the new product saying, 'Powershot definitely gives players a performance edge that allows them to focus harder for longer. I wish the product had been around when I was competing.'

- *Background knowledge and experience*: Reasonable (as a former international player, Jones arguably has some knowledge and experience about nutrition for performance. It is not known whether Wiles and Keating have good knowledge and experience of sports drinks).
- *Lack of apparent conflict of interest*: Poor (since Jones's club are benefiting from the sponsorship from Wiles and Keating, it is in Jones's interest to endorse the product).
- *Agreement with others*: Unknown.
- *Reputation*: Good (as club captain, Jones's reputation must be fairly good to be in that position. The reputation of Wiles and Keating is unknown).
- *Risk to reputation*: Reasonable (if Jones's claim turned out to be false then it may affect both her reputation as a former international player and the club's reputation. Wiles and Keating's reputation may be adversely affected if the claim turns out to be false).
- *Established procedures*: None.
- *Ability to give reasons*: Poor (no reasons are given as to the properties of the sports drink).
- *Careful habits*: Unknown.
- *Overall*: *credibility for claim is limited.*

d) An independent right-wing political blog has claimed that taxes will rise to cover the exorbitant costs of hosting the Olympics. It stated: 'Secret sources have admitted that the original estimates for hosting the Olympics were completely off target. The gaping black hole left in the finances will have to be covered by an increase in public taxes.'

- *Background knowledge and experience*: Unknown (more information as to the blog's authors would have to be collated in order for this to be assessed).
- *Lack of apparent conflict of interest*: Good (as it is stated that it is an 'independent' blog).
- *Agreement with others*: Unknown.
- *Reputation*: Unknown (more information as to the historical precedents set by the blog is needed).
- *Risk to reputation*: Limited (if the claim turned out to be false then it may lose readers, if it turned out to be true then it would gain in reputation and perhaps in political clout).
- *Established procedures*: Unknown (since the sources which provide the original information are unnamed).
- *Ability to give reasons*: Reasonable (the reason provided [that taxes will rise to cover the black hole in expenditure] is an acceptable one that has been used as a valid reason by politicians many times previously).
- *Careful habits*: Unknown (and is dependent on reputation from past claims).
- *Overall*: *credibility for claim is very limited.*

e) A coach for an under 15s rugby team confides in his regional manager that he suspects one of his players is suffering abuse at home. He then informs the child welfare manager and documents his concerns and the reasons he has for them, and ensures the document is kept confidential at all times.

- *Background knowledge and experience:* Good (assuming this coach is appropriately qualified for his position and has attended courses on safeguarding and protecting children).
- *Lack of apparent conflict of interest:* Good.
- *Agreement with others:* Unknown.
- *Reputation:* Unknown but given the position he holds, it would be reasonable to assume that his reputation is good.
- *Risk to reputation:* Reasonably high (if it was subsequently discovered that it was a malicious lie).
- *Established procedures:* Good (the established procedures issued by the governing body have been followed).
- *Ability to give reasons:* Good (the reasons for the claim required documentation).
- *Careful habits:* Unknown.
- **Overall: credibility for claim (that there is suspected abuse) is good.**

Learning Activity 4.5

a) An argument is good if the reasons given for the conclusion are true. – *TRUE (although it is also important to assess whether the argument is deductively valid too).*

b) Synthetic statements are those that are true by definition whilst analytic statements rest upon observation from experience. – *FALSE (analytic statements are true by definition, synthetic statements are true from experience).*

c) It is easy to verify the truth of a claim. – *FALSE (truth is a very slippery concept and ultimately all that can be made is a judgement).*

d) When assessing arguments it is important to highlight concepts or terms that might be contested. – *TRUE.*

e) Claims that are based on hearsay will always be false. – *FALSE (evidence from hearsay may be less likely to be true as a message can be distorted in the process but that does not mean it will always be false).*

f) Statistics provide conclusive evidence. – *FALSE (it is important to discover the underlying methods used to provide statistics before making a judgement as to their reliability. Even the best collected statistics will never prove something to be the case but merely indicate the likelihood of something being so).*

g) If a source's reputation is likely to be damaged if their claim is disproved then their credibility is enhanced – *TRUE (the more risk to a person's reputation, the less likely they are to make a bold or false claim).*

h) If someone has a conflict of interests then their credibility as a source will be reduced. – *TRUE.*

Chapter 5
Assumptions, generalisations and hypotheses

Learning Objectives

This chapter will help you:

- recognise assumptions;
- distinguish correlation from causation;
- define the method of induction;
- identify appropriate study samples and populations;
- understand what makes a good hypothesis.

The previous chapter considered whether an argument is a good one or not based upon its content; in other words, deciding whether there is good evidence for believing that the reasons or premises are true. This chapter will continue to focus upon evaluating the reasonableness of arguments and will consider identifying assumptions, the method of induction, deriving generalisations and forming hypotheses.

Assumptions

When the term 'assumption' is used in the context of arguments, it refers to an unstated claim or piece of evidence that the conclusion rests upon. The fact that it is implicit rather than explicit is what distinguishes it from being a reason. Most arguments in the real world contain assumptions as most arguments are not articulated as 'water-tight' deductive arguments such as those considered in Chapter 3. It is important, when analysing and evaluating arguments, that you are able to identify what assumptions are included in arguments, in order to decide whether the argument is a good one. For example:

> *Richard Gasquet was cleared to pick up the threads of his tennis career today when the sport's appeal against his assertion that he failed a doping test for cocaine on the grounds that it had been passed into his system from a nightclub kiss, was kicked out by the Court of Arbitration for Sport (CAS).*

> (Harman, 2009)

The conclusion of the argument in this paragraph is that Gasquet is able to restart his tennis career despite failing a doping test. The reason given is that the appeal against his claim that his doping failure occurred after cocaine passed into his body following a kiss was rejected. However, there are many other assumptions contained within this passage, including that Gasquet was a professional tennis player; that cocaine is an illegal substance in tennis; and that there is a set appeals procedure and associated body for dealing with doping cases. However, the most important assumption that underlies the argument making sense is that Gasquet successfully defended the original doping charge by claiming that the cocaine was only present in his body because of a kiss. Furthermore, there is an additional assumption that doping charges can be successfully fought on the grounds of the reasons for the substance being present.

Often, assumptions are so engrained into our understanding of events that we find it difficult to recognise or acknowledge them.

Assumptions as unstated reasons

Some arguments contain assumptions that are acting as reasons or an intermediate conclusion to an argument. For example:

Two 40-minute periods of exercise a week showed considerable improvements in fitness. Therefore if this was increased to three or four sessions per week, we should expect to see even greater improvements in fitness.

As it stands, this argument contains a single reason supporting a conclusion. However, there is no explicit reason that links this reason to the conclusion; it is based on an assumption. For this to be a deductively valid argument (see Chapter 3) it requires an additional reason and the assumption to be made explicit. The assumption here is that more exercise sessions equates to increased fitness levels. So this argument can be deductively expressed as shown in Figure 5.1.

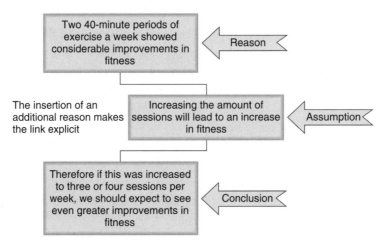

Figure 5.1.

Making an assumption explicit makes it easier to judge whether an argument is a good one. It also allows for a clearer and better debate on contentious issues and helps to avoid fallacious reasoning (see Chapter 6).

Learning Activity 5.1

Look at the following examples and decide what assumptions are being made.

a) Teachers often find that girls change their attitude towards PE lessons when they reach 14 or 15 years of age. Some people have claimed that this is due to peer pressure that promotes the view that sport is unfeminine.
b) 'The reason you sliced your shot was because you didn't follow straight through with your club.'
c) Taking a dive in football is a blatant example of cheating. It is an intentional act to deceive the official into thinking that a rule has been broken by the opposition.
d) Kitesurfing requires considerable power, strength and balance, not to mention the ability to read the ever-changing forces of nature in both sea and wind. For this reason, it is one of the most difficult and challenging sports in which to compete.
e) Michael Schumacher's return to Formula One has been criticised by some who have suggested that he will ruin the legend he created when he retired as the world's best driver and will only end up embarrassing himself.

Causation and correlation

One of the biggest assumptions that we make in our everyday reasoning is that of causation. That is, we create arguments that suggest there is a causal link between two events or occurrences. We saw this previously with the deductive 'if-then' arguments (Chapter 3) whereby we argued that if one thing happened, then another thing would also happen. One example that we used was, 'If Athavan is watching cricket, then it must be a Saturday.' If it really is the case that Athavan is watching cricket, then we can deduce that it is also a Saturday. However, the question arises as to how we reach this hypothetical 'if-then' argument in the first place. How do we discover that it is always the case that 'If Athavan is watching cricket, then it must be a Saturday'? One way is that we notice that two (or more) things always happen concurrently; it might be that every time we have known Athavan to be watching cricket, it has always been a Saturday. A famous example of these concurrent events was given by the philosopher David Hume who noticed that if one billiard ball strikes another, the other (previously at rest) will acquire motion away from the first. And the same concurrent events occur with other similar balls. The motion of one ball striking the other appears to cause the other to move. Hume called this apparent cause and effect the *constant conjunction*.

However, there are obvious differences between the cricket example and the billiard ball example. The relationship between the movement of two billiard balls is considerably stronger than the relationship between Athavan's cricket watching and it being a Saturday. In the former, the billiard balls are constrained by the laws of physics and have no free will of their own. In the latter, the relationship is much weaker; as an individual with free will, Athavan could choose to watch cricket on a Sunday, Monday or Tuesday. Equally, there may be no causal relationship at all, it might simply be correlational; that is, two things happen to occur at the same time but there is no direct relationship between them. In the cricket example it doesn't make sense to say that Athavan's cricket watching caused it to be a Saturday. The relationship between the two is indirect; it might be that Athavan only watches cricket on a Saturday because that is the only time the cricket is played, or it is the only day he has free from work. It is important not to confuse correlation with causation as there may be other factors involved in the relationship.

Learning Activity 5.2

Look at the following examples and decide whether you think it is likely that there is a causal relationship between the two things being described. Give reasons for your answer.

a) Out of 20 women who suffered serious knee ligament injuries, 15 of them sustained the injury in exactly the same period of their menstrual cycle.
b) Mark noticed that whenever he wore odd socks, he did really well in a competition.
c) No matter how hard a person hits a golf ball it always returns to the earth.
d) Whenever Justin ate and slept well leading up to a competition, he noticed he always performed to his target.
e) The majority of the country's lacrosse players went to private schools.
f) The majority of professional surfers have tanned skin.
g) Out of the three men standing on the winner's podium, two of them had brown eyes.
h) In a study that collected data from 200 schools, it was discovered that a significant majority of children who represented the school in sport had birthdays in the first half of the academic year.

Induction and generalisation

Identifying causal relationships is one way that we can gather information about the world. It also forms part of the method of induction. As was demonstrated in the previous chapter, deductive arguments take general information about the world to reach conclusions about specific instances. For example, if we accept the premise that 'All basketball players are tall and thin' (this is a general statement), and we know that 'Alex is a basketball player' then we can logically deduce something specific about the individual named Alex, namely that he 'is tall and thin'. Although deductive arguments can be useful in identifying whether conclusions logically follow from our premises (whether they are valid arguments), we need to construct and rely upon general statements in the first place. This is where the method of induction is useful. In contrast to deductive arguments, induction takes specific instances or observations we have about the world and derives general conclusions. In this sense, inductive generalisation goes beyond the information we already have in order to make assumptions about the wider world as a whole. However, whereas deductive arguments can be logically proven, inductive arguments rest upon much more shaky ground. As Hacking says in his excellent book on probability and inductive logic:

> *Valid [deductive] arguments are risk-free. Inductive logic studies risky arguments. A risky argument can be a very good one, and yet its conclusion can be false, even when the premises are true. Most of our arguments are risky.*

> (Hacking, 2001, p11)

Consider the following example:

> *A scientist studying muscle fatigue noticed that a sample of muscle taken from a subject following exercise showed a leakage of calcium. From this evidence she concluded that fatigued muscle leaks calcium.*

This is an inductive argument. It takes a specific instance (the fatigued muscle sample) and makes a generalisation that can be applied to all instances (all fatigued muscles). However, it is an extremely risky argument as it makes an enormous assumption based on a single piece of evidence. To illustrate, consider the following similar case:

> *Jack watched his first horse race and noticed that the jockey who was wearing a blue and white checked shirt won. From this evidence he concluded that jockeys who wear blue and white checked shirts will win horse races.*

Hopefully you will see that this is not a very good argument for the simple reason that making a generalisation about the winners of horse races based upon a single instance is not sufficient. It is easy to identify that Jack's argument isn't a good one because most of us have sufficient background knowledge about horse racing to know that it isn't dependent on the colour of a jockey's shirt. As such, I would feel pretty confident in saying that it would only take another race to show that Jack's generalisation was incorrect.

Let us return to the scientist who recognises that a generalisation based upon a single example isn't going to be taken seriously amongst her peers:

> *The scientist then repeated the test with twenty further samples and found that they too showed a calcium leakage. From this she concludes that a muscle sample taken from a subject following exercise will show a leakage of calcium.*

In this case, the scientist has repeated her experiment on more fatigued muscle samples. As the results are consistent with one another, the inductive generalisation she makes is much stronger than the one based on a single sample. But this begs the question, 'how many samples are needed to make a good generalisation?'

Sample and population

How many should I study?

Deciding how large your sample needs to be is very tricky as much of it is dependent on the total population size of what you are studying. It also is dependent on your background knowledge in the area. For instance, if you wanted to find out the weight of a test match cricket ball then you would only need to weigh one or two test match cricket balls to generalise to all test match cricket balls. This is due to the fact that the weight of a test match cricket ball will always be the same as it is a core part of the game (for instance, imagine what a test match would look like if the weight of a ball varied from game to game). However, if you wanted to make a generalisation about the weight of test match cricketers then a sample of one or two wouldn't be sufficient. We would be able to judge this based upon our background knowledge about humans and the requirements of cricket (in contrast to the weight of the ball, imagining a test match with cricketers who varied in weight would not affect the game of cricket itself).

However, there may be cases where we are trying to find out information and we don't have enough background knowledge to make an assessment about the size of the sample we need to test. In these instances, another method is often used. In these cases, we need to repeat our test until the results repeat themselves and a consistent pattern emerges.

Let us say that for marketing purposes we wish to find out the percentage of Arizona Cardinals supporters who are below the age of 18, between 18 and 35, and over 35 years. As they are going through the turnstiles we take a sample of 20 people. The percentages are 15 per cent, 55 per cent and 30 per cent respectively. We then take another sample of 20 people and find the percentages are 30 per cent, 45 per cent and 25 per cent. We take a further sample of 20 and find the percentages are 20 per cent, 50 per cent and 30 per cent. Eventually, the percentages will show a consistent pattern; say, 20 per cent, 55 per cent and 25 per cent, and we can be fairly confident that our sample size is adequate to eliminate any errors, and we know the age group upon which to target our marketing.

Who or what should I include?

In addition to sample size, we also need to ensure that our sample is a representative one and not biased towards a particular group that isn't representative of the sample as a whole. For instance, if we wanted to find out whether people would be willing to pay slightly higher taxes if they knew that this money would be ring-fenced for providing more after-school sports clubs, then conducting a survey at the local Conservative club would be highly likely to give a skewed perspective that wouldn't fully represent the total population, since the people who attend these clubs are likely to have fairly right-wing attitudes that wouldn't support these kinds of tax rises.

We must also be aware of our own prejudices and biases (see Chapter 1 for more information). An example of this can be seen in the case of a student who conducted a study into the effect of outdoor adventure activities on the confidence and self-esteem of disaffected youths. As an avid kayakist himself, he concluded that outdoor adventure activities have a significant positive effect on the self-esteem of these individuals and recommended that more activities of this type should be financed and provided as a result. However, his study did not take into account the effect of other things on the confidence and self-esteem of this group of people. Had he also studied or researched the effect of other activities, such as art, drama and music, he may have realised that it isn't the activity of kayaking itself, but other associated factors (such as being part of a small group, receiving individual attention and praise, setting and reaching achievable goals, etc.).

What are the relevant groups?

If we are making a generalisation then we need to ensure that all relevant categories or groups are included and no group that would make a difference to the accuracy of our generalisation is excluded. For instance, if we wanted to generalise about the amount of time people spend exercising per week, then the study would need to take into account all relevant groups of people, for instance, age, sex, socio-demographic, location; basically, any group that, if left out of our study, would falsify our generalisation. Therefore, asking 50 students studying sport and exercise and making a generalisation across the total population would not be sufficient. Ensuring that all relevant groups are accounted for is called stratification. For example, I knew a student who conducted an undergraduate study on the barriers to exercise by questioning people at his local leisure centre. He failed to see that he was asking his questions to an unrepresentative sample by conducting his research in this way, since those who were already using the leisure centre were least likely to have barriers. In this case, he was not including in his sample a very important population that was fundamental to his research question, that is, those who had significant barriers to exercise. See Figure 5.2 for an overview of areas to consider.

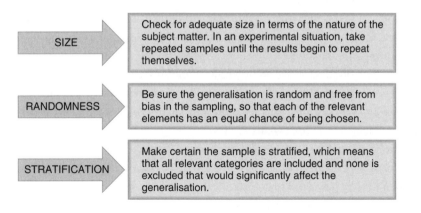

Figure 5.2.
(Adapted from Porter, 2002, p212)

Learning Activity 5.3

Decide whether the following generalisations are based on an adequate population and sample. Explain your reasons.

a) 'Most athletes go into debt to fund their sport.' Sample: 200 male students aged 18–24.
b) 'Watching sport decreases stress levels.' Sample: 10,000 males and females of various ages and health backgrounds from a diverse range of countries in all continents.
c) 'British girls often become disaffected with sport at around 14 years old.' Sample: 350 girls aged 10–18 who attend a state-funded comprehensive school in Norfolk.
d) 'Most people agree that fishing is a sport.' Sample: 18 people who were attending the national fly-fishing championships.
e) 'Premiership footballers are paid too much.' Sample: 3,000 men and women who were questioned in city shopping centres around the country.
f) 'Most adults take part in at least an hour of sport and exercise per week.' Sample: data gathered from the most recent national census.

The logical problem of induction

Although the method of induction and the subsequent generalisations we make appears to reap dividends for us by providing us with knowledge about the world, it is based upon an enormous assumption and therefore we can never be certain of the knowledge we get from using this method. It is a problem that has been of continual interest and debate amongst philosophers of science and is often referred to as Hume's logical problem with induction. The example often used to illustrate this problem is the case of the observed swan. Let us say that as we walk along a river, we see a pair of white swans. Several weeks later and in a different part of the country we note some more white swans, and then again, elsewhere we see a huge flock of swans, again all white. This develops our interest in studying swans and we eventually manage to observe and tag all known swans in the country, all of which, we discover, are white. As an authority on swans, the editor of a new website on birds asks us to add an entry describing a swan. Part of our description states that 'all swans are white'. This seems a very plausible generalisation since we have seen every known swan that lives in the country and they have all been white. However, shortly after our entry and on a trip to New Zealand we see a bird that looks exactly like all the swans we have seen before but it is black. Our generalisation has turned out to be false as it can plainly be observed that not all swans are white. We might for a time be persuaded that our generalisation is still fairly reasonable since out of the thousand swans that we have observed only one has turned out to be black. However, upon deciding to spend more time in New Zealand it is discovered that all the swans there are black and they outnumber the white ones we have seen back in England. Now we can no longer even generalise to say that the majority of swans are white. Furthermore, we cannot even be sure that the majority of swans are black either since it may be that in the rest of the world all swans are pink. The only way we could be sure of any generalisation would be to know the total number in the population and make sure that we had seen the majority of them. But then this creates a further problem since even if we were to know the total population of swans at a particular moment in time, we couldn't be sure that it would be the same for swans born in the future. And if we can't be sure of a swan's colour then perhaps we cannot be sure of any other characteristic in our description of a swan. In which case, where does this leave our ability to make a generalisation of any sort and how can we avoid making incorrect generalisations?

One answer to this is to be very careful and precise in using language. That is, if you have only observed a couple of instances of something then be very wary of generalising it to other instances. Even if you have carried out a research project with a large amount of data, then still be cautious in your conclusions, even if all your evidence (and statistical tests) supports a particular hypothesis. In particular make sure you steer away from using absolute terms such as 'This proves . . .' or 'It is a fact that . . .' etc. It is much better to use more cautious phrases such as 'The evidence, so far, strongly supports the hypothesis that . . .' Remember that the method of induction never proves anything, it only shows what has been the case to the best of your knowledge so far.

Case Study 5.1
Usain Bolt

An example of the inherent flaw in inductive reasoning was recently illustrated with the Jamaican sprinter, Usain Bolt.

A study published in a respectable journal (Uth, 2005) considered the issue of whether there was an optimum height and body mass for world-class sprinters. The author, Niels Uth, collected data from elite sprinters, made comparisons to the 'normal' population and concluded that the optimum height for sprinting was between 5ft 9in to 6ft 3in.

Uth states: 'All of the world-class sprinters were in the height range of 1.68–1.91 m (men) or 1.52–1.82 cm (women)' (p612). He then concludes: 'The fact that the sprinters' height data was normally distributed indicates that both very short and very tall stature may be disadvantageous for sprinters' (p612).

Uth conducted an inductive investigation. He took statistical data from all the all-time 100m top 50 lists and discovered that the height for elite sprinters fell into a particular range that could be differentiated from the range of a normal population. So far, we could say, the swan had always been white.

However 2009 saw the appearance of a black swan by the name of Usain Bolt. Bolt was 6ft 5in (1.96m) and beyond the boundaries dictated by the previous inductive reasoning. It led to a flurry of media speculation in an attempt to explain this anomaly (for instance, see Sports Life, 2009).

To be fair to Uth, despite media reporting to the contrary, nowhere in his paper does he suggest that elite sprinters must be within a particular height range. He does, however, state that it is very unlikely that a world champion will fall outside of this range. This claim may, in time, be falsified if all future world champions turn out to be outside Uth's optimum height range.

What this example illustrates is that we need to be careful in attaching too much weight to inductive evidence and the reasoning and consequences that we allow to follow.

Formulating hypotheses

The reason we often make generalisations is to understand, explain and predict the world around us. And as humans we are generally good at identifying and solving problems. However, solving problems requires our imagination and intuition as otherwise we would never know where to begin our investigations and experiments. This imagination and intuition about what is happening is formulated into what is known as hypotheses. Hypotheses are ways of speculating about the relationship between known facts. For instance, if we notice that the players that get the least amount of injuries are those that spend the most amount of time working on their core strength, then we can hypothesise that strong core muscles are important in injury prevention. From this hypothesis we can work out the best way of conducting an investigation to see if our theory is correct.

Often our hypotheses come from our own experience. A colleague of mine who was both a sports person and a drummer noticed that he became just as exhausted from drumming as he did from running. Although the literature suggested otherwise, from his own observations he developed the hypothesis that elite-level drumming is much more cardiovascular intensive than was stated in the literature available. This hypothesis enabled him to conduct experiments that suggested that the previous literature on the requirements of drumming was inaccurate and had led to an inappropriate generalisation (it was later discovered that the original literature was based upon an experiment conducted in the 1920s and on a particular style of drumming that wasn't comparable to rock and pop drumming).

Developing a good hypothesis

The formulation of hypotheses is important if we are to understand the world around us and make cases and justification for action. However, if we are not to waste time, effort and money, then we need to ensure that the hypotheses we come up with get as close to the truth as possible. So, how do we know which hypotheses are good ones and which ones we should avoid or discard? The philosopher, Thomas Kuhn, came up with five elements that make for a good hypothesis (1977). These were: accuracy, consistency, simplicity, fruitfulness and scope. However, here I will use five of Porter's (2002) categories, which are: consistency, plausibility, comprehensiveness and simplicity but I will change his last one, predictability, to testability.

Consistency

A new hypothesis should fit into our current understanding of the world, in much the same way that a new piece of the jigsaw will fit into the puzzle. There may of course be times when a new piece of evidence causes us to re-evaluate our whole picture of the world (as happened in the Copernican revolution, which changed our understanding of planetary orbits, and also in our understanding of skill acquisition, which moved from a schema model to a more evolutionary/perception and action coupling model) but, generally, a hypothesis should make sense when considered alongside other things we believe to be true. For example, if I developed a hypothesis that muscle mass increases with the amount of lettuce a person consumes then it would go against my other knowledge about the composition of muscle and lettuce. If I already accepted that muscle requires protein in order to develop and that lettuce does not contain significant amounts of protein then to develop a hypothesis that states muscle mass increases with lettuce intake is not consistent with this knowledge.

Plausibility

In addition to ensuring our hypotheses are consistent with our other beliefs, we should also ensure that they are plausible. That is, our theories should make sense in the light of traditional and accepted knowledge. For example, to hypothesise that our team is losing games because a voodoo witch doctor has cast a spell on them doesn't fit with our scientific world view about causation. This explanation is implausible compared with others, such as the team being depleted through injury, or having an inadequate game plan that doesn't represent the team's strengths and the opposition's weaknesses. Similarly, if we hypothesise that balls fly through the air by being carried on the backs of fairies, then this hypothesis is implausible if our world view is one that accepts the laws of physics.

Comprehensiveness

A hypothesis needs to provide the fullest explanation possible. In other words, it should attempt to account for all the evidence not just small pieces. For example, if we wanted to account for why cricket is played in Pakistan then it would not be sufficient to produce a hypothesis that stated that it was due to being a product of British colonialism, as this would not account for why cricket is not played to the same extent in other former British colonies such as Canada and Singapore. Nor would it be sufficient to simply say that it was introduced by a Lieutenant called Edmund Smith in 1851 (which, as far as I know, is not true) because that wouldn't account for its growth and popularity. Any hypothesis about why cricket is played in Pakistan needs to take account of all the reasons for its introduction, development and popularity and not just a couple of reasons.

Simplicity

There is a principle in formulating hypotheses that is called Ockham's razor and it states that 'entities should not be multiplied beyond what is required'. This means that we should adopt the most simple explanation for the phenomenon rather than make it any more complicated than is necessary. If, for example, we wanted to work out why we were unsuccessful in our attempt to kick a ball at a target, then explaining it by tracing a series of events back to a butterfly's movement in Canberra is creating an over-complicated theory. A much more sufficiently simple hypothesis would be to say that we hadn't accounted for a change in wind direction when we kicked the ball. Creating an adequate balance between ensuring that the hypothesis is simple enough to explain the phenomenon being studied but also comprehensive enough to account for all the evidence is a difficult trick to master.

Testability

One of the purposes of formulating hypotheses is to predict future events. We should be able to judge our hypothesis as being good or bad on the accurateness of its predictions. The philosopher

Karl Popper said that the best hypotheses are those that are most open to being tested and yet still resist attempts to be proved wrong. He called this 'falsifiability'. If, for example, I hypothesise that the team that spends the most money on players at the beginning of the season will win the league, then I will only need to wait until the end of the season to find out if my hypothesis was a good one. If my hypothesis proves to be correct over several seasons then I can judge that my theory is a good one since it is open to testing and yet still hasn't been proved wrong. This is in contrast to non-falsifiable statements such as: 'The Scarlets will one day be considered the best team in the world.' Not only does it contain ambiguous terms such as 'best', which could mean 'most popular', 'most dominant', 'most successful', etc., but also this hypothesis is impossible to prove false as the timescale is unlimited. Even though the Scarlets haven't been considered the best team in the world yet, there is always the possibility that they might in future. This, therefore, is not a good hypothesis since it doesn't form a prediction that is able to be tested. The best hypotheses are those that can be readily tested and are open to falsification. See Figure 5.3 for an overview.

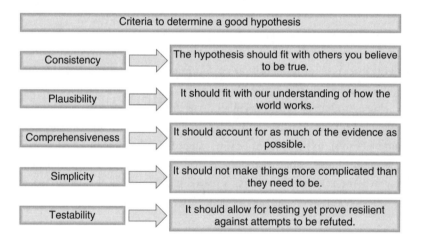

Figure 5.3.

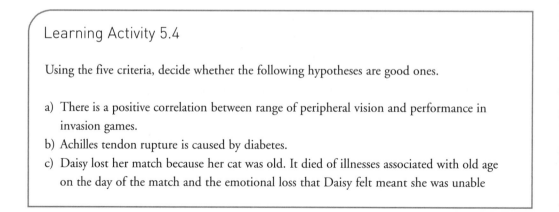

Learning Activity 5.4

Using the five criteria, decide whether the following hypotheses are good ones.

a) There is a positive correlation between range of peripheral vision and performance in invasion games.
b) Achilles tendon rupture is caused by diabetes.
c) Daisy lost her match because her cat was old. It died of illnesses associated with old age on the day of the match and the emotional loss that Daisy felt meant she was unable

to fully concentrate on the game itself, which led to a decreased level of performance. This resulted in losing points to her opposition, which led to the loss of the match.

d) There will come a time where athletes will regularly be jumping over 10m in the high jump.

e) Project72, which provided sport-related opportunities for 14–18 year olds in the town of Market Rasen, had a significant impact on reducing teenage anti-social behaviour in the area over the two-year period it ran.

f) Nathan's sporting success is determined by the gods he prays to before every fight. Sometimes they give him the strength and power to win, other times they seek to instil humility by allowing him to lose.

This chapter has considered how we gain primary evidence to support our claims. In particular it touched upon arguments that often rest upon unstated assumptions, the concept of causation, and the methods of induction and generalisation. However, I have only been able to provide the briefest overview of some very deep and complicated issues. There is a lot more to be said about generalising from data collected, particularly about the use of statistics and probability. For more information in these areas, see some of the resources listed in the further reading section at the end of this chapter.

Test Your Understanding

Learning Activity 5.5

State whether the following statements are true or false.

a) An assumption is generally an implicit statement contained within an argument.

b) Correlation is the same thing as causation.

c) The method of induction is able to derive certainty.

d) Induction is forming a generalisation from specific instances.

e) An adequate research sample needs to be at least 50 per cent of the total population.

f) An adequately stratified sample means that all groups that might significantly affect the results are included in the data.

g) A 'black swan' is the term used when a new piece of evidence contradicts our previous inductively-based knowledge.

h) Forming a good hypothesis requires knowledge and imagination.

i) A good hypothesis needs to be testable.

Chapter Review

What is an assumption?

An assumption is an implicit statement contained within an argument. It may underlie a basic reason, function as an additional reason or function as an intermediate conclusion.

What is the difference between correlation and causation?

Correlation suggests a link between two or more things, i.e. that when A is present, B will also be present. However, this does not necessarily mean that A causes B or that B causes A as they may both be the consequence of something else, e.g. sweat and reddening of the skin may both be present but one does not cause the other; rather they are the effect of increased body heat.

What is meant by induction?

Induction is the method of reasoning from a particular set of instances to a general conclusion. For instance, if on observing several occasions that the cause of a flat tyre was a puncture, I may generalise that all flat tyres are caused by punctures. I may of course be wrong in my generalisation and this is why the method is considered risky.

What is a sample and population?

In order to minimise the risk of making an incorrect generalisation, appropriate testing is required. The amount of times you test something is called the sample or population. In the same way that a sample of cloth should show you what the whole cloth would look like, a study sample should be representative of your whole population and enable you to make an accurate generalisation without testing everything or everyone.

What is a hypothesis?

A *hypothesis* is an unproven or unestablished theory or idea about the way the world is.

What is a value judgement?

A *value judgement* is a subjective ranking of one thing to be of higher or lower worth than something else. For example, if I am debating whether boxing should be banned, the argument may come down to the value judgement that I make that places individual liberty over protection from harm.

Further Reading

Bonnett, A (2001) *How to Argue: A Students' Guide.* Harlow: Pearson Education Limited. ★★★☆☆
This students' guide is designed to help facilitate students' written work (although there is also a chapter on oral arguments). It is a very readable textbook that offers an adequately thorough

examination of key concepts, and provides exercises, examples and case studies. It is particularly refreshing to see a chapter dedicated to cultivating original thought – something that too often is neglected in academic teaching.

Fisher, A (2001) *Critical Thinking: An Introduction.* Cambridge: Cambridge University Press.
★★★★☆

This is an excellent introduction to critical thinking that focuses upon providing opportunity for the practice and improvement of critical thinking skills. It covers all aspects of critical thinking, from a discussion as to its worth and value, to using the tools of critical thinking in decision making, but its main attribute is the wealth of practical exercises, examples and answers it utilises, which makes it an excellent self-directed learning resource.

Hacking, I (2001) *An Introduction to Probability and Inductive Logic.* Cambridge: Cambridge
University Press. ★★★★☆

Ian Hacking is considered an authority on probability and inductive logic and the depth of knowledge that he has in this area is demonstrated by his ability to introduce and explain clearly some very complicated issues. The book itself is well presented and contains many sections and subsections, which makes it easy to skip to the relevant section. It also contains a wealth of examples and exercises. For an introduction to this area, it is highly recommended.

Porter, BF (2002) *The Voice of Reason: Fundamentals of Critical Thinking.* Oxford: Oxford University
Press. ★★★★☆

The aspect that sets this apart from other books on critical thinking is that it approaches critical thinking from a very philosophical perspective. It is divided into three distinct sections: language and thought, systematic reasoning, and modes of proof, all of which are discussed in an intelligent but accessible way and provide examples, exercises and partial answers. An appealing addition to the text is the inclusion of cartoons and dialogue to illustrate and highlight the point being made.

Taleb, N (2008) *The Black Swan.* London: Penguin. ★★★★★

Taleb's 'black swan' stems from Hume's logical problem of induction, i.e. our predisposition to generalise from a limited number of observed cases and then believe that this generalisation will enable us to predict future cases. As the eminent philosophers Hume and Russell (amongst many others) indicated, there is no logical reason why this should be so. This is an excellent book that I would recommend to all those interested in the more philosophical problems associated with the method of induction.

Thomson, A (2003) *Critical Reasoning: A Practical Introduction* (second edition). London:
Routledge. ★★★★☆

This is a seminal text and an accessible guide to the practice of critical thinking. It contains thorough explanations and practical exercises that range from short paragraphs to longer passages of argument. Some of the examples have become slightly dated (such as the BSE controversy) although other examples are still relevant (such as the classification of cannabis) but overall, the examples remain useful in highlighting the way that argument (and the underlying assumptions that it rests upon) is really used in the public sphere.

Answers to Learning Activities

Learning Activity 5.1

The following suggestions are not definitive.

a) Teachers often find that girls change their attitude towards PE lessons when they reach 14 or 15 years of age. Some people have claimed that this is due to peer pressure that promotes the view that sport is unfeminine. – *Assumptions: That peer pressure is more intense or affects 14- and 15-year-old girls more than at other ages. That 14- and 15-year-old girls do not want to be doing or seen to be doing something that is unfeminine.*

b) 'The reason you sliced your shot was because you didn't follow straight through with your club.' – *Assumption: An unsliced shot requires a straight follow through.*

c) Taking a dive in football is a blatant example of cheating. It is an intentional act to deceive the official into thinking that a rule has been broken by the opposition. – *Assumption: The definition of cheating is an intentional act to deceive an official into thinking that a rule has been broken by the opposition.*

d) Kitesurfing requires considerable power, strength and balance, not to mention the ability to read the ever-changing forces of nature in both sea and wind. For this reason, it is one of the most difficult and challenging sports in which to compete. – *Assumption: That kitesurfing is a sport. That a difficult and challenging sport requires the things mentioned (power, strength . . .). Perhaps that not everyone is able to be successful at it, or certainly not without hard work and practice.*

e) Michael Schumacher's return to Formula One has been criticised by some who have suggested that he will ruin the legend he created when he retired as the world's best driver and will only end up embarrassing himself. – *Assumption: That it is wrong for Schumacher to return to Formula One racing. That those who return to sports after retirement will not be successful. That legends (or reputations) are tenuous.*

Learning Activity 5.2

The purpose of this learning activity was to get you to think about how we reach judgements about causation. As such, the answers are just my suggestions and are not definitive.

a) Out of 20 women who suffered serious knee ligament injuries, 15 of them sustained the injury in exactly the same period of their menstrual cycle. – *Although more information is needed as to the sample this was taken from, there is other corroborative scientific evidence that suggests levels of a hormone affects elasticity of ligament, which results in a greater risk of injury when undertaking particular activities. If this evidence is reliable then it doesn't mean that the point in a menstrual cycle causes a ligament injury, since the process is much more complicated than that. It simply explains a possible relationship between the two things.*

b) Mark noticed that whenever he wore odd socks, he did really well in a competition. – *Although many people have these kinds of superstitions, there is no evidence to suggest that the wearing of odd socks and athletic performance are related. There may be a psychological reason why Mark performs well (see the placebo effect) but the cause for good performance is not found in the socks themselves. This is a case where correlation should not be mistaken for causation.*

c) No matter how hard a person hits a golf ball it always returns to the earth. – *The relationship between a ball and the earth can be found in physics and the law of gravity. The very fact that it is called a 'law' presupposes that it remains constant and that balls will always return to the earth when hit.*

d) Whenever Justin ate and slept well leading up to a competition, he noticed he always performed to his target. – *There seems to be reasonable scientific evidence to suggest that nutrition and rest affects athletic performance, which is in contrast to the odd socks example.*

e) The majority of the country's lacrosse players went to private schools. – *The way that this is phrased in terms of events in time suggests that going to a private school affects whether a person plays lacrosse (i.e. private school happens first, playing lacrosse occurs second – and not the other way around). However, understanding a causal relationship here requires background knowledge of lacrosse and private schools. If evidence is found that private schools are significantly more likely to teach lacrosse than state schools, then it could be reasonably assumed that a person has a greater chance of becoming a lacrosse player if they go to a private school as they would be more likely to have an opportunity to play it. However, it would not be appropriate to say that private schooling causes someone to play lacrosse in the same way that gravity causes the ball to fall to earth. It simply means that there is a higher probability they will go on to play lacrosse in the future.*

f) The majority of professional surfers have tanned skin. – *In contrast to the previous example, this statement doesn't contain any notion of time; it simply identifies a correlation (professional surfing and tanned skin). To make a judgement about causation requires background knowledge. For instance, since surfing is an outdoor water sport, and tanned skin occurs through exposure to the sun's rays, it is more likely that the activity involved in surfing will lead to a tan than the activities involved in getting a tan will lead to surfing.*

g) Out of the three men standing on the winner's podium, two of them had brown eyes. – *Similar to the previous example, this states a correlation between two things (being on the winner's podium and having brown eyes). However, it would be rash to suggest that there is a causal relationship between the two. Not only is there a lack of known evidence suggesting eye colour is related to athletic success but the sample on its own is too small to make a generalisation.*

h) In a study that collected data from 200 schools, it was discovered that a significant majority of children who represented the school in sport had birthdays in the first half of the academic year. – *In contrast to the previous example, this sample size is much bigger and therefore provides more reliable evidence on its own, even without corroborating evidence from elsewhere. However, to decide whether one thing causes the other (e.g. date of birth causes athletic representation) requires further investigation. There could be many other factors involved in this phenomenon, such as self-confidence, assertiveness, height and weight, which aren't themselves directly affected by date of birth but rather are more dependent on the way that the school year is structured.*

Learning Activity 5.3

a) 'Most athletes go into debt to fund their sport.' Sample: 200 male students aged 18–24. – *This sample is far too narrow to make such a generalisation. It needs to be larger and include women, other age groups and non-students.*

b) 'Watching sport decreases stress levels.' Sample: 10,000 males and females of various ages and health backgrounds from a diverse range of countries in all continents. – *This is a large sample (though still only accounts for a tiny fraction of the world population) and importantly includes a varied and representative sample of both sexes, different health backgrounds and nationalities. Therefore it would seem reasonable to make such a generalisation.*

c) 'British girls often become disaffected with sport at around 14 years old.' Sample: 350 girls aged 10–18 who attend a state-funded comprehensive school in Norfolk. – *Although the sample size and age group are reasonable, Norfolk might not be representative of the whole of Britain.*

d) 'Most people agree that fishing is a sport.' Sample: 18 people who were attending the national fly-fishing championships. – *The sample size is far too small and the group questioned are biased since they are already attending what is named a sporting event.*

e) 'Premiership footballers are paid too much.' Sample: 3,000 men and women who were questioned in city shopping centres around the country. – *This is a fair sample size, represents both sexes and since they were questioned at shopping centres, it should provide the views of a diverse range of people.*

f) 'Most adults take part in at least an hour of sport and exercise per week.' Sample: data gathered from the most recent national census. – *As the national census is a government document that citizens are legally obliged to complete, it provides a reliable and broad-based sample.*

Learning Activity 5.4

a) There is a positive correlation between range of peripheral vision and performance in invasion games. – *This is a reasonable hypothesis. It is both testable and fits with our hypotheses and knowledge about the world.*

b) Achilles tendon rupture is caused by diabetes. – *This is a plausible hypothesis that can be tested but it isn't comprehensive enough as we already know that an Achilles tendon rupture can be caused by things other than diabetes. This hypothesis needs to be rephrased to take this knowledge into account, e.g. 'Achilles tendon rupture can be caused by diabetes.'*

c) Daisy lost her match because her cat was old. It died of illnesses associated with old age on the day of the match and the emotional loss that Daisy felt meant she was unable to fully concentrate on the game itself, which led to a decreased level of performance. This resulted in losing points to her opposition, which led to the loss of the match. – *This hypothesis is far too complicated. A much simpler formulation would be sufficient, e.g. 'Daisy's loss could be explained to a large degree by the emotional effect of her cat's death earlier that day.'*

d) There will come a time where athletes will regularly be jumping over 10m in the high jump. – *This hypothesis isn't testable as it provides no specific time span. There is always a possibility that it may be true sometime in the future.*

e) Project72, which provided sport-related opportunities for 14–18 year olds in the town of Market Rasen, had a significant impact on reducing teenage anti-social behaviour in the area over the two-year period it ran. – *This is a reasonable hypothesis. It provides a specific period of time over which the official crime figures for the area can be compared with the figures for when the project wasn't running.*

f) Nathan's sporting success is determined by the gods he prays to before every fight. Sometimes they give him the strength and power to win, other times they seek to instil humility by allowing him to lose. – *This is a poor hypothesis in that it is not open to testing as both winning and losing a fight supports the initial hypothesis itself. I would also maintain that, although Nathan's belief in the gods may have a psychological effect on his performance, the idea of the gods themselves determining success is implausible and contradicts other knowledge about how the world works.*

Learning Activity 5.5

a) An assumption is generally an implicit statement contained within an argument. – *TRUE.*

b) Correlation is the same thing as causation. – *FALSE (just because two or more things appear to happen at the same time does not mean that one is causing the other).*

c) The method of induction is able to derive certainty. – *FALSE (relying on inductive methods will always be taking a risk as there may be a time where the generalisation is shown to be false).*

d) Induction is forming a generalisation from specific instances. – *TRUE.*

e) An adequate research sample needs to be at least 50 per cent of the total population. – *FALSE (the sample needs to be appropriate to the type of thing that you are studying. Sometimes one or two instances are sufficient, sometimes it requires tens of thousands and more).*

f) An adequately stratified sample means that all groups that might significantly affect the results are included in the data. – *TRUE.*

g) A 'black swan' is the term used when a new piece of evidence contradicts our previous inductively-based knowledge. – *TRUE.*

h) Forming a good hypothesis requires knowledge and imagination. – *TRUE (forming good hypotheses requires the imagination to see links between things you already know to be the case).*

i) A good hypothesis needs to be testable. – *TRUE.*

Chapter 6
Evaluating arguments: fallacies

This chapter will help you:

- identify flaws in short passages of reasoning;
- understand what is meant by a fallacy;
- become familiar with the names given to specific fallacies.

By now you should have the tools to be able to construct and evaluate good arguments; however, you also need to be able to identify the tricks and techniques that are often used to promote viewpoints and conclusions that are flawed yet may appear at first glance to be persuasive. An argument based on erroneous reasoning is called a *fallacy* and many are common enough to have their own particular names. This chapter will identify some of the most common fallacies and provide case studies and learning activities to help you detect them in passages of argument.

Learning Activity 6.1

Look at the following examples and decide where errors in reasoning have been made.

a) Everyone knows that footballers get paid a fortune for just kicking a ball around whilst nurses get paid a fraction of that and are saving people's lives. Therefore, all footballers should be forced to donate some of their income to help nurses.

b) Those that live in northern England are more likely to suffer from bad health than their southern counterparts. Bad health has been associated with lack of exercise. Therefore those in the north of England are exercising less than those who live in the south.

c) The reason why women's sport doesn't get much coverage on television is because no-one wants to watch it. It's just a fact that men's sport is much more exciting to watch.

d) There's nothing wrong with cheating if you can get away with it. Everyone else does it so that means it's fine.

e) If we allow athletes with prosthetic limbs into able-bodied events then before you know it, all we'll be doing is testing the technology and not natural human ability.

Identifying flaws in reasoning: fallacies

Being able to note where an argument breaks down is an essential skill in critical thinking. An argument that appears, at first glance, to be sound but is actually flawed is called a fallacy. It is a deceptive or misleading argument that is based on false reasoning. This chapter outlines some of the most comment flaws that occur in arguments. It is not a definitive list by all means (see the further reading section at the end of this chapter) and some of the fallacies described are only distinguished by a subtle difference, but it attempts to provide a reasonable overview of some common mistakes.

Emotive language: using rhetoric

Sometimes an argument can appear persuasive simply due to the rhetoric or language that is used. Rhetoric is the art of using language persuasively. That is not to say that rhetoric is always used with malicious motives, for a rhetorical device in itself is neither good nor bad, it is merely a persuasive tool. Nevertheless, one ought to be on guard in assessing arguments for rhetorical ploys that present an argument in a way that makes it appear to be stronger than it actually is. One common way of attempting to persuade an audience is through using emotive language. This has the effect of bypassing the rational part of the brain to trigger an emotional reaction that will predispose the receiver to believe something is the case when there are perhaps no good reasons for believing it to be so. Good orators are experts in the use of rhetoric and are common in the arenas of politics, war and sport. They have an ability to draw others to their cause and persuade them to act in particular ways, sometimes even persuading people to sacrifice their life on the basis of a particular belief or ideology.

Learning Activity 6.2

An example of the effective use of rhetoric can be seen in the film *Any Given Sunday* where the coach, Tony D'Amato (Al Pacino), inspires his failing team to victory. Part of his speech contains these words:

We are in hell right now . . . and we can stay here . . . or we can fight our way back into the light. We can climb out of hell. One inch at a time . . . On this team, we fight for that inch. On this team, we tear ourselves, and everyone around us, to pieces for that inch. We CLAW with our finger nails for that inch. 'Cause we know when we add up all those inches that's going to make the difference between WINNING and LOSING between LIVING and DYING . . . Now I can't make you do it. You gotta look at the guy next to you. Look into his eyes. Now I think you are going to see a guy who will go that inch with you. You are going to see a guy who will sacrifice himself for this team because he knows when it comes down to it, you are gonna do the same thing for him. That's a team, gentlemen and either

●●●▶

> *we heal now, as a team, or we will die as individuals. That's football guys. That's all it is.*
> *Now, whattaya gonna do?*
>
> (*Any Given Sunday* (1999) O. Stone (Dir.). USA: Warner Bros.)
>
> Read the above excerpt and try to identify why it is a powerful and persuasive speech. What language does it use and what emotions does it affect?

In the example depicted in Learning Activity 6.2, rhetoric has a fairly innocuous use. Yet there are many instances whereby the use of rhetoric is much more iniquitous. An attempt to play on the emotion of fear is a common rhetorical ploy, as is language that appeals to novelty, compassion and sexiness (Figure 6.1). This is particularly common in advertising or marketing that is designed to sell a particular product, and the language is often implicitly contained within pictures or images.

Four common rhetorical ploys	
Appeal to fear	**Appeal to novelty**
E.g. 'If we do not win today, jobs will be on the line and contracts up for renewal. You don't want to be the one who winds up unemployed.'	E.g. 'You should buy these football boots because they contain the latest technology and will be available in these colours for a limited period only.'
Appeal to cuteness or sexiness	**Appeal to compassion, pity or guilt**
E.g. 'Are you single and lonely? Then sign up to our specifically designed fitness program to give you a body that will have guys and girls falling at your feet to ask you out on a date.'	E.g. 'Teaching football to these impoverished third-world children gives them enjoyment in an otherwise bleak life, but it is only possible with your generous donations.'

Figure 6.1.

Intimidating or obscure language

Another linguistic ploy that speakers may use is to deliberately present information in a language that is inaccessible to the lay-person in order to make it sound more authoritative, and therefore better, than it really is. This includes acronyms, technical or outmoded language, or 'buzz words'. For example:

Our mawkish conception of the values of sport need to be oppugned. We need to consider a new way of thinking about PEDs as we can't rely upon GBs to make appropriate decisions since they are already held hostage to the political will in this sycophantic system.

Often when speakers use intimidating or obscure language it is in attempt to disguise a lack of knowledge and understanding of issues, for arguably, those that understand their subject well are able to articulate it in a way that enables other to understand. However, there is also a responsibility on you, as the audience, to uncover what is really being said, as it may be that the speaker/writer is addressing an audience on the assumption that they possess knowledge to a particular level. That is, it would not be feasible for the speaker to always spend time clarifying foundational knowledge if they are limited by time/space to give an argument that is built upon this knowledge. Nevertheless and as a general rule, in presenting an argument you should always try to articulate your ideas as clearly as possible, and in assessing the arguments of others you should be suspicious if they appear to be deliberately using language in an intimidating or obscure way.

Using connotative language

Our choice of words can be effective tools of persuasion simply because they contain implicit and hidden meaning (connotations). For example:

> *Mark was a true hero who stepped into the ring to fight patriotically for his country against the stooge of the repressive Soviet ideology. The fight saw our boy courageously dodge and weave his way to victory despite the often under-hand and cowardly attempts by the Russian to lay a knockout blow.*

If the speaker is addressing a partisan audience then it is easy to revert to utilising language that supports the audience's given mindset. In this instance, 'our boy' is labelled a courageous and patriotic hero, words which have a positive connotation, whilst the Russian is labelled an under-hand and cowardly 'stooge of the repressive Soviet ideology', which presents him in a negative way. The way we describe things affects our understanding and perception of them. This type of connotative language is quite common in arguments and we need to be sensitive to it.

Giving language agency

As illustrated, words are human tools. However, they have no motivation, intention, beliefs or agency of their own. So it is a fallacy to suggest that abstract words and symbols can act in particular ways. For example:

> *Fair play insists that we do not allow commercial enterprise to dictate the direction of the game. If we allow the game to be run by multinational corporations then it will result in a very uneven playing field for those clubs that are left behind.*

This fallacy seems to be a common mistake within student essays. Students often treat abstract words and phrases as if they have the same conscious thoughts that we as humans have. In the example above, the concept of fair play does not insist anything; people who wish to uphold the ideals of fair play (whatever they are deemed to be) are the ones who are doing the insisting rather than the concept itself. In the same vein, commercial enterprise doesn't dictate anything, but rather this is done by boards of directors in charge of those commercial enterprises. Sometimes it is tempting, for reasons of brevity, to use words and concepts in place of longer, more specific phrasing, but it is important for the sake of accuracy that language is used with as much clarity as possible.

Deriving 'ought' from 'is' (and the naturalistic fallacy)

The essence of this fallacy is to take certain facts about the world and from those facts make a judgement about what 'ought' to be the case. It derives from the Scottish philosopher David Hume's observation that when people make ethical judgements they begin from a position whereby they make statements of fact then (almost imperceptibly) leap to making statements of value. An example of this would be the following argument:

> *Boxing causes brain damage and often draws in young, ill-educated people from deprived*
> *backgrounds. Therefore, boxing should be banned.*

This, as an argument, jumps from statements of fact ('causes brain damage' and 'drawing in young, ill-educated people from deprived backgrounds') to a statement of value ('boxing should be banned'). However, there is nothing that explicitly links the conclusion to the premises. The argument could be strengthened by including additional premises that state what is wrong with causing brain damage and drawing in young, ill-educated people from deprived backgrounds but it would still fall foul of Hume's criticism.

Along similar lines, the naturalistic fallacy was coined by another British philosopher, G.E. Moore, who noted that ethical statements about what is good and bad, for instance, were often (unjustifiably) defined via the use of natural properties, such as, what is desirable, pleasant, enjoyable or healthy. So for instance, if we state that 'Swimming is healthy' then we commit the naturalistic fallacy if from this statement we conclude that 'Swimming is good.'

Attacking the person (or *ad hominem*)

If a response to an argument is to make an attack on the person giving the argument rather than to attack what is being said, then it is to commit the *ad hominem* fallacy. So for example:

> *How can our Physical Education teacher lecture us about the importance of keeping fit? Look at*
> *her – she's overweight and obviously does no exercise herself!*

In this example, no attempt is made to deal with the argument itself, that is, the one on the importance of keeping fit, but rather the attack is directed towards the person who is making that argument.

'So are you!' (*Tu quoque!*)

This is related to the *ad hominem* fallacy as it accuses the person making the argument of the very thing that they are arguing against. In essence, it is to say that the person proposing the argument is being logically inconsistent or hypocritical. For instance:

Caroline says that she supports animal welfare and yet she spends her weekends participating in cruel sports; hunting foxes and shooting pheasants.

This isn't necessarily a fallacy as it is often used a tool to undermine a person's credibility. However, in the above example, it would be considered a fallacy if it could be demonstrated that Caroline is not being contradictory; for Caroline may well support the welfare of animals such as horses and dogs whilst regard foxes as vermin and pests, and pheasants as food (in the same way that many others view cows, pigs, sheep and chickens). This example makes the assumption that supporting animal welfare is inconsistent with the activities of hunting foxes and shooting game, in the same way that not all those who wish to protect animal welfare are vegetarians. As is relevant in many debates, it all depends on what you mean by particular terms, and in this case, what is meant by 'animal welfare'.

Slippery slope

This is to argue that if you allow one thing to happen it will inevitably lead to other (more negative) things; hence, once you begin sliding down a slippery slope it is very difficult to regain one's footing and stop. Sometimes this fallacy is also called the 'thin end of a wedge' in that it is very difficult to draw a line and justify it as some will always want to push it that little extra. An example of this would be the following:

If we allow one foreign player in the game then before we know it others will follow and the league will be overrun with non-native players. Soon our national team would have to be drawn from those in the lower leagues and we'd be a laughing stock on the international stage.

This argument makes the assumption that allowing one foreign player would inevitably lead to an influx of others. It is based on hypothetical causal reasoning when there is no evidence that this would be the case. The slippery slope argument often plays on the emotion of fear and, as such, can generally appear to be quite persuasive. If the 'slippery slope' argument were as problematic as its proponents would believe, we'd never be able to make any decision for fear of sliding to the bottom. This fortunately isn't the case and there are many instances where a line is drawn without it leading to other unpalatable consequences. For instance, the claims made in the above example could be seen over time to be unfounded. It may have been the case that the introduction of foreign players into the game resulted in the league being more appealing to watch and therefore more profitable. As some of this profit was then channelled into the game at grassroots level it increased the skill development and opportunities given to home-grown players who then successfully represented their country. One of the problems with the 'slippery slope' argument is that it deals with future possibilities and one can only make a judgement on these predictions with the benefit of hindsight. When assessing whether what appears to be a 'slippery slope' argument is fallacious or not, you need to consider whether there is any good evidence for reaching the conclusion and whether there has been a precedent set in similar occurrences.

Beg the question

This fallacy is to argue a case by assuming it in the first place. For example:

> *Manchester is a city that is proud of its sporting heritage; it is a city that is prepared to invest in much-needed sporting facilities and provide opportunities to all its citizens. It is not a city that fritters hard-earned tax-payers' money on pointless projects that only benefit a few. That is why we should support the development of this new stadium.*

In this example, an assumption is being made that the new stadium falls into the former category (a much-needed sporting facility that will provide opportunities to all) and not the latter (a pointless project that only benefits a few). However, no argument is given to support this assumption and it begs the question as to why the stadium is considered a much-needed sporting facility rather than a pointless development.

Building a straw man

A straw man is something that is fragile and can easily be knocked down (in contrast to a real man). The fallacy of building a straw man refers to the way that someone's argument can be misrepresented in order to give the impression that your own argument is stronger than it is. For example:

> *Skate-boarders argue that they should not be banned from skating in public spaces. They think that they should be given special consideration over other groups of people, including the elderly who would have to give up benches and other places to sit so that skate-boarders can use them for their own activities.*

This type of argument is a 'straw man' since it misrepresents the opposing view. Arguably, skate-boarders who want access to public spaces do not wish to be given special consideration and do not wish to prevent vulnerable populations, such as the elderly, from being able to use the spaces too.

Here's another example:

Andrew: 'You need to start training more if you want to be selected for the team.'
Luke: 'Why am I the one who has to have a perfect training record? Other people get selected and they're not always at training.'
Andrew: 'No I didn't say that at all. I just said that you have to train more than you currently do.'

In this example, Luke deliberately misrepresented Andrew's position in order to make his own argument stronger, as he was arguing on the basis of consistency and fairness in that Andrew wasn't treating him fairly when compared with others. The fallacy of a straw man can often be the cause of many real disagreements and heated arguments and it is important to watch out for them so that you aren't drawn into an argument in which you are set up to lose.

The best arguments are those which attempt to create the strongest counter-arguments and yet are still able to identify the flaws contained within them. Creating simplistic counter-arguments in an attempt to strengthen your own is a weak and cowardly ploy.

Appeal to authority

In the previous chapter, one way of assessing credibility was to judge the knowledge and experience of the person making the claim. If it is deemed that the person has a degree of expertise in the area then their credibility is enhanced. However, sometimes relying on the knowledge of someone in authority can be fallacious especially when they have a conflict of interest or they are simply using their position of authority as the reason to accept their claim without other verification. For instance, 'expert witnesses' in the British courts have suffered a torrid time recently as the credibility of their statements has been reconsidered in the light of successful appeals. Although Western society doesn't seem to be quite as deferential to authority as it has been previously, those in positions of power, and the claims they make, are still respected simply because of the authority they hold. For example:

> *This new isotonic sports supplement has been scientifically proven to enhance performance and aid recovery. Tested and endorsed by our best scientists, this product is at the cutting edge of sports nutrition.*

This claim is an appeal to authority as it uses the label 'science' and 'scientist' to enhance its credibility. No further information is given as to how the research was carried out or how the results have been interpreted; rather the claim rests simply upon the audience's respect for science and scientists.

Appeal to tradition

Despite what we might sometimes think, humans are generally very conservative creatures. For reasons of efficiency, laziness or perhaps just pure dogmatic habit, we will often follow a familiar course of action. The result of this means that we sometimes defend our actions simply on the grounds that, 'we've always done it like that' no matter how irrational or absurd they may be. Consider the following example:

> *Sports such as bear baiting and cock fighting have been around for hundreds, if not thousands of years. It is part of our heritage and therefore not something that a bunch of liberal do-gooders have any right to attack.*

The premise of this argument is that simply because bear baiting and cock fighting have been around for a long time, it is morally acceptable. As such, this argument falls foul of the naturalistic fallacy by saying that because something is traditional it means that it is therefore 'good'. There may be an argument to be had about whether and why traditional practices should be valued and preserved but merely appealing to tradition is not sufficient in itself.

Creating a false dichotomy

A false dichotomy is to suggest that there are only two particular choices or outcomes when there may be many others. False dichotomies are often effective because they create simplicity by presenting issues in black and white terms. For instance:

> *If we allow the use of genetic technology in sport then we will be faced with a load of mutant athletes as a result. Either we take a hard line on the issue or see the end of sport as we know it.*

This is arguably a false dichotomy since there are (will be) many applications of genetic technology and few (if any) of them will create what we might emotively call 'mutant' athletes. Furthermore, it is debatable whether sport as we know it will end, since sport itself is a human construct and will exist as long as humans participate in and create rules for it. To depict the complex issue of genetic technology in sport in this way is to over-simplify it and to neglect important considerations and aspects.

Over-generalisation

It is sometimes quite tempting to increase the force of your argument by making an assumption that there is more evidence for your reason than there actually is. Consider the following example:

> *Everybody knows that Layne Beachley is the greatest female surfer ever.*

The trouble with this argument is that it makes a false generalisation (see Chapter 5 on generalisation for more on this). It is not true that *everybody* knows this; it might be the case that many people who are interested in the surfing world would agree with this statement, but stating that everybody knows it is simply false. Here is another example:

> *Most people agree with me that snooker does not warrant a place on prime-time television.*

Even using slightly subdued language does not render this a reasonable statement to make unless there is good evidence to suggest that it is the case. If you happen to have only asked a few of your friends (who share similar views to you) then even if they all agree with the statement, it would be fallacious to generalise out to the wider population.

A good critical thinker (who believes it important to preserve the virtues of honesty and truthfulness) will not set out to deliberately deceive or exaggerate claims in an attempt to persuade her audience. In this then, it is important to use language cautiously and to only make generalisations when there is good reason to do so.

Here are some important things to remember about making generalisations (Figure 6.2).

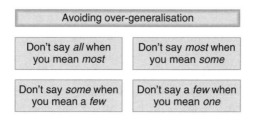

Figure 6.2.

Lies, damned lies and statistics

The phrase 'lies, damned lies and statistics' is often attributed to the English prime minister Benjamin Disraeli (although there is some dispute as to whether he was the one who originally coined it) but it seeks to illustrate the way that statistics can be used as a tool of (illegitimate) persuasion. Consider, for example, the following:

> *Nine out of ten people questioned said that they prefer CoreClimaCool products.*

If you are told that nine out of ten people would use a particular product, it gives the impression that the product is worth having. Yet, this statistic neglects other important information. The first question that needs to be asked is 'is the sample representative?' If they are employees of the firm that makes the product, and their salary rests upon its sales then they have a vested interest in endorsing the product and the results cannot be generalised out to a wider population. A second, similar, question is, 'how many people were asked?', for the larger the sample, the more likely it is that the results are judged to be valid (although there are philosophical problems associated with this method of induction as highlighted in the previous chapter). If one million people were questioned and 900,000 people said they preferred the product then it carries a much greater statistical power than if only ten people were asked and nine of them preferred it. A third question that needs to be considered is 'what comparison is being made?' If the question that was being asked was, 'Which would you prefer: a CoreClimaCool product or being locked in a cage with a hungry lion?' then it is unsurprising that the vast majority of them would prefer the former (in this instance, it would be more surprising that one in ten would prefer the lion but then perhaps this one person is a lion tamer, an adrenaline junkie or mentally insane). The point being made here is that it is very easy to be persuaded by numbers without knowing what they actually mean or where they come from.

The gambler's fallacy

This fallacy refers to a situation whereby we draw a false conclusion from the world of probabilities. For instance:

The coin has landed heads for the previous four times, therefore it has a much greater chance of landing tails next time.

If there is an equal chance at the outset of the coin landing heads or tails then no matter how many times the coin is tossed and lands heads, it *still* has a 50 per cent probability of landing heads next time. Although this can be quite complicated to explain, in essence, you need to consider the total number of possible combinations for times that the coin has been flipped, not the probability for that particular pattern (i.e. four consecutive heads: a 1/16 chance) occurring. So, out of five coin tosses, there is equal probability of tossing 'heads, tails, tails, tails, heads' or 'tails, heads, tails, heads, heads' as there is in tossing 'heads, heads, heads, heads, tails'.

Here's another example:

Faye: 'I'm putting £50 on Villa to win this weekend.'
Rich: 'What! They've lost their last five games!'
Faye: 'Yeah I know but if you look at their previous results they always win half of their games and finish mid-table. Since they've lost their last few games and are languishing at the bottom of the table they're definitely due for a win.'

Here, Faye is neglecting the fact that there may be other factors involved in a team's success. It may be that Villa lose the rest of their games and are relegated at the end of the season despite finishing mid-table for the previous few seasons. (This is also related to the problem of induction that was highlighted in Chapter 5.)

The reverse gambler's fallacy is when you believe that there is a bias for a particular outcome, i.e. the predominance of heads, when the probability of either remains equal.

It is claimed that we have a psychological disposition to fall for the gambler's fallacy; one of the reasons being because we neglect the fact that the sample we bear witness to is only a small fraction of a larger, more representative sample that averages out in the long term (in the abstract world of probabilities).

Learning Activity 6.3

Identify the fallacies in the following examples.

a) Following their recent cup match, Dave Bellam of Whitney Colts ridiculed the opposition's claims that they were fielding unregistered players. He said, 'How they can suggest such a thing is beyond me when they were caught last season having played two unregistered players. They are the ones that the officials need to keep their eye on.'

b) The IOC will be setting a dangerous precedent if they allow darts to be in the Olympics. Before too long, people will be campaigning for snooker and poker to also be included and the Olympics would turn into a farce that would only be serving the needs of beer-drinking, gambling louts rather than the showcase of athletic talent that it ought to be.

c) The funding of leisure centres is an important issue in local politics. The taxpayer has always subsidised leisure facilities and therefore should continue to do so in the future.

d) We are a proud nation that always endeavours to do the right thing. Therefore I ask you to support this wonderful opportunity that we have to hold the Olympic Games that will live up to the ideals of our society.

e) Our top research scientists conducted a study to investigate the relationship between weight distribution and medial ligament tears. They found that 75 per cent of injuries to the knee were suffered following acute weight transference from one leg to the other.

f) Everyone knows that people suffer terrible things in closed societies: you only have to look at the way athletes were forced to take steroids and train extensively in the Eastern European states during the Cold War. As Cuba is a closed society run by a dictator it only follows that its athletes must be forced to do things that they would otherwise wish not to do.

g) Henry's handball was yet another example of cheating at the top level. Professional players have too much at stake to play fairly and unfortunately match officials are not always going to be able to spot infringements of this type especially in a crowded goal mouth. Either we introduce goal-line technology or we will see this type of cheating happen all the time and the game will go to ruin.

Test Your Understanding

Learning Activity 6.4

State whether the following statements are true or false.

a) Fallacies are a form of bad argument.
b) Rhetorical ploys are persuasive because they appeal to an emotion or audience's bias.
c) The use of rhetoric is morally unacceptable.
d) It is acceptable to use acronyms and technical jargon when your audience is familiar with their meaning.
e) Attacking the person not the argument they make is called *ad hominen*.
f) '*Tu quoque!*' is to suggest that the person making the argument lacks credibility.
g) To make a deliberately weak counter-argument so you can knock it down easily is to create a straw man.
h) The 'slippery slope' fallacy is an argument that suggests unforeseen consequences will follow from an action.
i) It is never acceptable to appeal to authority in arguments.
j) It is important to know where statistics originate from before using them in arguments.

Fallacy	Brief description
• Rhetorical ploy	Attempting to persuade by appealing to the emotions, biases or prejudices of the audience
• Over-generalisation	Exaggerating the evidence to appear more forceful than it is
• Deriving 'ought' from 'is'	Deriving a value or moral judgement from empirical evidence
• *Ad hominen*	Attacking the person making the argument rather than the argument itself
• *Tu quoque*	Avoiding the issue and accusing someone of the thing that they are accusing you
• Slippery slope	Suggesting that one thing will inevitably lead to another
• Beg the question	Assuming the very thing you are arguing for in the first place by using your conclusion as a reason to support itself
• Building a straw man	Creating a weak counter-argument in order to knock it down easily and make your own argument look strong
• Create a false dichotomy	Maintain that there are only two possibilities (when alternatives might be available)
• Misleading statistics	Deliberately use unreliable statistics to support an argument

Figure 6.3.

Chapter Review

What is a fallacy?
A fallacy is a bad argument. It is 'any trick of logic or language which allows a statement or a claim to be passed off as something it is not' (Pirie, 2006, pix). An overview of fallacies is given in Figure 6.3 opposite.

Further Reading

Hamblin, CL (1970) *Fallacies*. London: Methuen. ★★☆☆☆
Although the aim of this book is to demonstrate how the study of fallacies has been neglected from texts on logic, what Hamblin does best is to illuminate the way that fallacies have been considered and developed from a historical perspective. However, what is most striking about this book is that despite its original and engaging content, it is unlikely to appeal to the average undergraduate student, simply because of the aesthetic limitations of a book last published almost 40 years ago.

Paul, R and Elder, L (2004) *The Thinker's Guide to Fallacies: The Art of Mental Trickery and Manipulation* (fourth edition). Dillon Beach, CA: The Foundation for Critical Thinking. ★★★☆☆
This title is part of the Critical Thinking Foundation's miniature guides and for the small amount of space it occupies, it covers a lot of content. One of the primary focuses of the book is to highlight the importance of intellectual integrity in winning arguments. As such, the authors' aim is to dissuade students from deliberately choosing to use one of the 44 types of fallacy outlined within it.

Pirie, M (2006) *How to Win Every Argument: The Use and Abuse of Logic*. London: Continuum. ★★★★☆
Containing an A to Z description of 80 different fallacies, this is a comprehensive reference guide to bad reasoning. It provides several examples to illustrate the fallacies explained and also includes an appendix that classifies the fallacies into five different types.

Tindale, C (2007) *Fallacies and Argument Appraisal*. Cambridge: Cambridge University Press. ★★★★★
This is a recent and welcome detailed consideration of fallacious argument. It categorises fallacies into their various types and explores them in an interesting and engaging way. As well as covering the usual linguistic and logical fallacies, it also provides chapters for fallacious reasoning based on quantitative and statistical research. It also helpfully provides practice exercises for each chapter as well as suggested further reading.

Warburton, N (2000) *Thinking from A to Z* (second edition). London: Routledge.★★★☆☆
This is essentially a dictionary of argument so that one is able to quickly and easily look up a term or phrase to discover its meaning. It also gives helpful examples to illustrate the use of difficult concepts. It particularly highlights many of the fallacies that are used in bad arguments such as the straw man, slippery slope, *ad hominem* and appeal to authority.

Answers to Learning Activities

Learning Activity 6.1

a) Everyone knows that footballers get paid a fortune for just kicking a ball around whilst nurses get paid a fraction of that and are saving people's lives. Therefore, all footballers should be forced to donate some of their income to help nurses. – *There are two criticisms that can be made about this argument. First, it suffers from a false generalisation, since it is not true that all footballers get paid a lot of money; it is just a few at the top of the game. The counter-argument is that it is only a minority of footballers (the Premiership 'superstars') who earn significant wages. Many professional and semi-professional footballers earn considerably less and have a shorter career span than many other occupations. Second, there is also no obvious step between the premise and the conclusion; there is an implicit premise that it is unfair that footballers should earn more than nurses (due to what their jobs entail) and that to compensate for this disparity footballers should be forced to give up some of their earnings to nurses.*

b) Those that live in northern England are more likely to suffer from bad health than their southern counterparts. Bad health has been associated with lack of exercise. Therefore those in the north of England are exercising less than those who live in the south. – *Although bad health has been associated with a lack of exercise, it has also been associated with other things such as poor diet, poverty, lack of education, etc. The difference between the north and the south could have been caused by any, or a combination, of these things.*

c) The reason why women's sport doesn't get much coverage on television is because no-one wants to watch it. It's just a fact that men's sport is much more exciting to watch. – *The problem with this argument is that it might be getting things the wrong way around. It could equally be argued that no-one wants to watch women's sport because it doesn't get much coverage on the television. The second sentence supports the reason given but provides no further supporting evidence; it simply states it as 'fact'.*

d) There's nothing wrong with cheating if you can get away with it. Everyone else does it so that means it's fine. – *This argument is flawed because it uses the reason that 'everyone does it' to mean that therefore it is acceptable. Unless you accept a kind of morality based upon the actions of the majority (if it is the case that 'everybody does it', which again, is a generalisation) then there is no reason to assume that it makes it morally acceptable. Furthermore, it could be argued that there is something inherent in the definition of cheating that makes it morally wrong.*

e) If we allow athletes with prosthetic limbs into able-bodied events then before you know it, all we'll be doing is testing the technology and not natural human ability. – *This is making an assumption that allowing the use of prosthetic limbs will inevitably lead to the use of other technology, which will lead to further technology and so on. It is called the 'slippery slope' fallacy.*

Learning Activity 6.2

This speech is persuasive because it appeals to the emotions of pride, honour and solidarity. It successfully plays upon an individual's desire to belong to a group and to be well regarded within that group. The language used is of life and death, heaven and hell; a dichotomy of consequence, one good and one bad. From this, comparisons are made between winning a football game and winning in life. However, when considered under more sober analysis the relationship between the two is not as clear as is implied by D'Amato. Losing the match will not lead to death or a life of eternal hell, after all, it's only a game; rather, one could claim that the attempt to sacrifice everything one has in order to win the match may be more likely to lead to death or a life of suffering through injury. In this respect, it falls under the fallacy of *creating a false dichotomy*. Nevertheless, as an inspirational team talk, it serves its purpose of inspiring the team to victory.

Learning Activity 6.3

a) Following their recent cup match, Dave Bellam of Whitney Colts ridiculed the opposition's claims that they were fielding unregistered players. He said, 'How they can suggest such a thing is beyond me when they were caught last season having played two unregistered players. They are the ones that the officials need to keep their eye on.' – *This commits the fallacy of 'tu quoque!' as it doesn't address the issue but rather just accuses the other person of being guilty of the same thing.*

b) The IOC will be setting a dangerous precedent if they allow darts to be in the Olympics. Before too long, people will be campaigning for snooker and poker to also be included and the Olympics would turn into a farce that would only be serving the needs of beer-drinking, gambling louts rather than the showcase of athletic talent that it ought to be. – *This uses the 'slippery slope' fallacy as it suggests, without reason, that one thing (allowing darts) would inevitably lead to another (a farce).*

c) The funding of leisure centres is an important issue in local politics. The taxpayer has always subsidised leisure facilities and therefore should continue to do so in the future. – *This is appealing to tradition in maintaining that just because the taxpayer has subsidised leisure facilities in the past, it is a consequence that they should in the future. Arguably it also falls foul of the naturalistic fallacy in reaching an ethical judgement from an empirical fact.*

d) We are a proud nation that always endeavours to do the right thing. Therefore I ask you to support this wonderful opportunity that we have to hold the Olympic Games that will live up to the ideals of our society. – *This is rhetorically persuasive because it flatters the audience in being morally virtuous and then uses this flattery to support a recommendation. It also 'begs the question' by making an assumption that holding the Olympic Games will be doing the right thing.*

e) Our top research scientists conducted a study to investigate the relationship between weight distribution and medial ligament tears. They found that 75 per cent of injuries to the knee were suffered following acute weight transference from one leg to the other. – *This appeals to authority and also to the power of statistics. Merely because they are labelled 'our top research scientists' does not say how qualified these people are, for they may be very lowly regarded scientists relative to other companies and institutions. The label 'scientist' carries a connotation of being a credible source but again there is no further evidence given in support of this view. Finally, the statistic used does not give enough information to make a judgement as to the reliability and validity of this data. Questions need to be asked as to the size and scope of the sample, and what other variables were measured and controlled.*

f) Everyone knows that people suffer terrible things in closed societies: you only have to look at the way athletes were forced to take steroids and train extensively in the Eastern European states during the Cold War. As Cuba is a closed society run by a dictator it only follows that its athletes must be forced to do things that they would otherwise wish not to do. – *First, this passage makes a generalisation that 'everyone' knows something to be the case when this is unlikely to be so. Following this generalisation, it labels both Eastern Europe and Cuba as 'closed societies' and then makes further assumptions as to the characteristics they share (e.g. the way they treat their athletes).*

g) Henry's handball was yet another example of cheating at the top level. Professional players have too much at stake to play fairly and unfortunately match officials are not always going to be able to spot infringements of this type especially in a crowded goal mouth. Either we introduce goal-line technology or we will see this type of cheating happen all the time and the game will go to ruin. – *This commits the fallacy of creating a false dichotomy. There might be several alternatives to introducing goal-line technology that will not mean that the game will go to ruin.*

Learning Activity 6.4

a) Fallacies are a form of bad argument. – *TRUE.*

b) Rhetorical ploys are persuasive because they appeal to an emotion or audience's bias. – *TRUE.*

c) The use of rhetoric is morally unacceptable. – *FALSE (Rhetoric itself is not morally problematic for it can be used for good and bad; it is the purpose behind using rhetoric that is a moral consideration).*

d) It is acceptable to use acronyms and technical jargon when your audience is familiar with their meaning. – *TRUE (Be empathetic with your audience and treat them accordingly).*

e) Attacking the person not the argument they make is called *ad hominen*. – *TRUE.*

f) '*Tu quoque!*' is to suggest that the person making the argument lacks credibility. – *NOT SPECIFICALLY (Although it may undermine their credibility as a consequence, technically it is to avoid addressing the issue itself and simply accuse the other person of what they have accused you).*

g) To make a deliberately weak counter-argument so you can knock it down easily is to create a straw man. – *TRUE.*

h) The 'slippery slope' fallacy is an argument that suggests unforeseen consequences will follow from an action. – *FALSE (It is to suggest that the consequences of an action can be foreseen).*

i) It is never acceptable to appeal to authority in arguments. – *FALSE (As we saw in the previous chapter, appealing to a credible source is one way of making a reasonable judgement. However, using an appeal to authority merely as a rhetorical device (when perhaps you know that the authority is not as credible as the rhetoric suggests) is a morally questionable act).*

j) It is important to know where statistics originate from before using them in arguments. – *TRUE (As outlined in Chapter 1 regarding the dispositions of a critical thinker, we ought to ensure that our arguments are based on as reliable reasoning as possible).*

Chapter 7
Evaluating arguments: examples

Learning Objectives

This chapter will:

* consolidate some of the theory provided in the previous chapters;
* illustrate how to assess longer passages of argument;
* provide an opportunity to evaluate a longer piece of reasoning.

The preceding chapters have explained some of the theory behind the construction and evaluation of arguments. This chapter will demonstrate how that theory can be put into practice in the deconstruction and evaluation of longer passages of argument.

When faced with an argumentative piece of reasoning, it is important to first get the gist of what is being said and to identify the main argument that is being presented. Then you can start to analyse and evaluate the detail. The summary shown in Figures 7.1 and 7.2 might help.

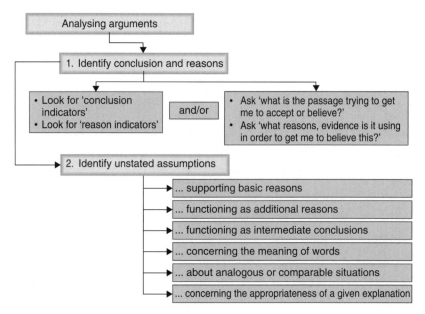

Figure 7.1.

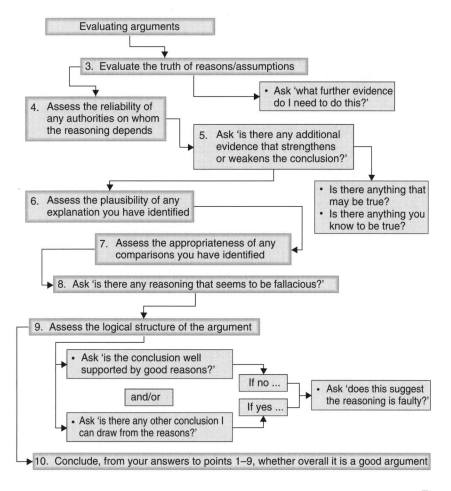

Figure 7.2.
(Adapted from Thomson, 1996, pp99–100)

The following example is an article taken from the *Independent* newspaper. The analysis and evaluation that follows is intended to be used as an illustration of how to dissect and evaluate the arguments being made. It does not cover all the issues raised in the article and does not provide a definitive (if it is possible to have one) assessment. Nevertheless, it still provides a fairly detailed and comprehensive appraisal.

Case Study 7.1
The London Olympics are failing their racial promises: time to make sure the Games are what Mandela believed they could be.

Good for you, I say to Trevor Phillips and the Equality Commission who may investigate the London Olympics Organising Committee (LOCOG) because its leading lights are near-replicates of Seb Coe, the Tory chair. Our medal-winning athletes and players are multiracial but at the top, it is still a white man's game; jobs, contracts, positions of influence are going, of course, to the lucky boys' club.

The official website was down at the weekend – perhaps they are blacking or 'womaning' up some of the smug faces. The only ill-fitting stranger let in appears to be Dr Bari of the discredited Muslim Council of Britain, which tells you a lot. Oh, and Princess Anne. Think of it as the latest divvying up of fiefdoms in our long history, courtiers, Dukes and Barons grabbing assets. The Cavaliers back, feathers and all.

What makes it unconscionable is that our capital was sold and won on 'diversity' by Ken Livingstone and Tessa Jowell – who really did mean it. But that promise has been cynically archived. Partly because Conservatives are now running the show and partly because few have called the chiefs to account, until now. They didn't really mean any of it – surely only fools were taken in?

Then the Tories joined in the clappy chorus singing hymns to London's all-sorts. Why, even Michael Howard joined in, he who gave us the campaign poster 'It is not Racist to Impose Limits on Immigration'. This same politician waxed lyrical in 2004: 'Over 300 languages spoken by 200 communities here – London would be able to welcome athletes like no other city on earth. Every athlete would feel an element of their own home touching them in London.' Feeling bilious? Come join me around the bucket.

Perfidious Albion does it again, and again and again, deceitfully undertakes whatever she needs to on behalf of her avaricious sons and then, without a beat or a flash of contrition, bins the pledges and runs with the winnings. If it wasn't so self-important and unprincipled itself, the Olympic Committee might have said something, asked why the contents are not delivering what the label clearly describes, indeed brandishes

Walk around the four host boroughs: Newham, Hackney, Waltham Forest and Greenwich. Sit in cheap old cafés and talk to ordinary people, men and women of all races who have never seen much of glittering, billionaire London. Bit by bit, and irreversibly, like skin, the shine is fading, worry lines have appeared, hope turned sallow. Some are angry, most resigned and fatalistic. That's Blighty for you.

In our country, citizens either accept that the born-to-rule always will, or even more alarmingly, condemn as unpatriotic those of us who tirelessly object to privilege passed on from father to son. Cue bloggers who will fly into intemperate, filthy rages and call for my ungrateful head. The ranters reveal their own pathetic insecurities. Inexplicably, the most raucous upholders of the status quo are people who have everything to gain if we had real equality. That's Blighty for you.

Backing the EHRC are Operation Black Vote, whose head, Simon Woolley, warned last spring that black and Asian businesses were not getting a look-in as contracts were being handed out by Coe and co. Gary Nunn of the gay campaign group Stonewall says there is very little evidence of 'real new work or sporting opportunities for disabled people, black people and gay people'.

Last month, LOCOG once again issued meaningless gobbledygook to reassure sceptics. Their head of diversity, Stephen Frost, who worked for Stonewall, said equality and diversity would be 'championed'. Yeah, right.

Actually, I exaggerate. Enthusiastically working for one thriving sector of the forthcoming games is a real cross-section of our Metropolis. The army of volunteers welcomes 'ethnics' and other unfortunates through the back door, lackeys proud to serve their nation for nothing. That, says LOCOG, shows how the organisation is 'fully reflective of London'.

Then there are the sports stars of all backgrounds, many of them using talent and prowess to prove themselves in an unfair society. (I don't believe many Eton boys get these medals.) A number of the medallists are now knights and dames of the realm. They could embarrass LOCOG by speaking out. Ain't heard a squeak of dissent from them. Too busy going to gala events, I guess, or delivering feel-good messages for advertisers.

Time to wake up, make sure that the Games are what Nelson Mandela believed they could be when he backed our bid: 'There is no city like London, wonderfully diverse and open'. So, Lord Coe, what happened next? Please explain and in detail.

[Alibhai-Brown, 2009]

1. Identify conclusion and reasons

The main claim that Alibhai-Brown makes is encapsulated in the title: 'The London Olympics are failing their racial promises'. In other words, the London Olympic Games were supposed to promote diversity and yet, so far, have failed to do so. The reasons given to support this claim are:

- one of the reasons for the success of the London Olympic bid was its focus on diversity;
- that the Equality and Human Rights Commission (EHRC) may investigate the London Organising Committee for the Olympic and Paralympic Games (LOCOG);
- that the majority of the board members of LOCOG are white men;
- and that contracts for providing the Olympics are not being awarded to local businesses.

2. Identify unstated assumptions

The main assumption underlying the latter three reasons is that they have a direct relationship to the claim that the Olympics isn't living up to its promises. In particular, underpinning the first reason is the assumption that the possibility (for it is only stated as a possibility) of the EHRC investigating LOCOG means that the Olympics are not living up to their 'racial promises'. Equally, the second and third reasons make the assumption that the constitution of board members and the awarding of contracts have a direct relation to the Olympic promises on diversity.

3. Evaluating the truth of reasons/assumptions

When attempting to verify many of the claims that the article makes I eventually found what I presume is the piece that motivated Alibhai-Brown to write her commentary. This was an article written by Jamie Doward on the day previous to Alibhai-Brown's text and was published in the

Observer newspaper (Doward, 2009). In essence, many of the claims and sources that Alibhai-Brown cites are originally given in Doward's piece and it appears that Alibhai-Brown takes them as being true on trust rather than undertaking her own research and subjecting them to corroborative testing.

The initial claim stated in the article's title is clarified later on in the text when it suggests that one of the reasons that London won the bid for the 2012 Olympics was due to the emphasis it placed upon diversity. There is a general consensus of opinion that agrees with the view that the success of London's bid was in part due to the multicultural values held across Britain and in London in particular (as can be verified by comments by Trevor Phillips of the Equality Commission, a letter by government minister Ben Bradshaw, as well as claims made by members of the London Organising Committee itself) and so this claim ought to be accepted as true. The more controversial claim is that these original aims and ambitions regarding diversity are not being fulfilled in practice.

This claim may be supported by the reason given in the first paragraph that the EHRC are considering investigating LOCOG. Although this was reported in Doward's article, he doesn't provide the source for his claim and I couldn't find any further evidence that this claim was true. The only related evidence I could find was by searching the EHRC's website, which showed that they had previously commissioned reports into whether the Olympic Development Agency are doing enough to promote diversity. The fact that a precedent has already been set may suggest that another investigation will occur but it doesn't necessarily mean that an investigation supports Alibhai-Brown's conclusion. However, regardless of the truth of this reason, it does not necessarily support the conclusion. Such investigations may be routine quality assurance processes for these types of projects, or the commission may be statutory obliged to investigate complaints of whatever nature (though this does not necessarily mean that the complaint will be upheld).

Another reason Alibhai-Brown provides to support her claim is that the board of the Olympic Organising Committee do not demonstrate the diversity of population that underpinned the London bid. Alibhai-Brown states that only one member of the LOCOG board is non-white and only one is a woman. The official LOCOG website verifies this and so provides good evidence for Alibhai-Brown's claim. Alibhai-Brown provides further criticism of the board's exclusive membership by denigrating these two non-white-male members. One she labels as 'discredited' whilst the other is mocked for her heritage. The truth of this reason therefore seems fairly well supported although this does not necessarily mean that those implementing the Games are failing in their 'racial promises'. Nevertheless there is some evidence that could provide support for this claim, and this comes from an article written by Trevor Phillips (of the Equality Commission) when London was first awarded the Olympics. He states:

> *London's victory is more than just a great marketing job. It is a recognition that our capital offers the best real-world answer that humanity has to the challenge of ethnic and religious diversity. It was reflected in the team we saw promoting the London bid. Whilst others wheeled out a phalanx of grey middle-aged suits, our line up paraded humanity in all its glorious diversity . . . London, as Sebastian Coe reminded us time and again, was offering the world a Games that showed us the future as it could be.*

(Phillips, 2005)

Admittedly, the group representing the London bid is not the same thing as the board that organises the Games but it does suggest that a view was promoted that the Games would reflect diversity throughout its operation and that would include those facilitating and directing at the top.

That LOCOG is committed to diversity is widely supported. Ben Bradshaw, Minister for Culture, Media and Sport, wrote to Neil Kinghan of the EHRC verifying this. He states: 'LOCOG's commitment to diversity and inclusion will, it hopes, be a large part of the legacy it leaves behind for the private sector' (Bradshaw, 2009). LOCOG itself continues to assert its commitment to diversity. For instance, a blog post written by LOCOG's government relations manager, Craig Beaumont, frequently cites evidence of the company's support for diversity in the development of the London Games: 'Only this week, LOCOG was the first winner of the "Gold Standard" from Diversity Works for London, and we are the fastest organisation in the UK to achieve the Equality Standard for Sport' (Beaumont, 2009).

Support for Beaumont's claim can be found on the London Development Agency's website in a press release on 18 December (London Development Agency, 2009). Diversity Works for London (DWfL) is a mayoral enterprise set up to promote diversity in businesses in London. It provides resources for business to become more appealing to those populations and groups that might have been physically, culturally or psychologically barred from working within these organisations. Achieving the Gold Standard means that a business has demonstrated good diversity practice across six strands (including age, disability, ethnicity and sexual orientation). How hard it is to achieve the Gold Standard or its real worth is difficult to assess. One thing that may undermine its credibility is the fact that it relies upon self-assessment (though the results are corroborated by DWfL). Nevertheless, this does provide evidence against Alibhai-Brown's suggestion that LOCOG is 'unprincipled' and her implication that it is overtly discriminatory against non-whites.

The fourth main reason given for Alibhai-Brown's claim is that local businesses that are representative of the diverse London population are not being given contracts for Olympic projects. She cites (what appears to be) direct observational evidence:

> *Walk around the four host boroughs: Newham, Hackney, Waltham Forest and Greenwich. Sit in cheap old cafés and talk to ordinary people, men and women of all races who have never seen much of glittering, billionaire London . . . Some are angry, most resigned and fatalistic.*

Evidence that may support this claim comes from a copy of EHRC's research report 6 which was published in August 2008 (Smallbone et al., 2008). It highlights several relevant findings in relation to Alibhai-Brown's argument; in particular, that the Olympic Development Agency (ODA) is showing evidence of attempts to increase supplier diversity on Olympic related contracts but that they are constrained by existing UK and European legislation as to how much they are able to favour target groups (including local business and minority groups) over other suppliers. As an example of the ODA's attempts, the report cites the 'CompeteFor' website that is being used as a vehicle to attract these target groups and ensure diversity. The report nevertheless acknowledges that successfully ensuring diversity in developing and hosting the Olympic Games will be a challenge and one that can only really be addressed through central government departments and policy decisions.

Although this report does support Alibhai-Brown's claim that local businesses are not successfully competing for contracts, it does provide a defence against her assertions of an endemic race prejudice within the Olympic Organising Committee itself. The report maintains that problems promoting diversity are not due to a lack of desire by the ODA but rather are due to a variety of conflicting pressures and interests.

4. Assess the reliability of any authorities on whom the reasoning depends

The great majority of the sources used and quoted in Alibhai-Brown's article come from Doward's piece in the *Observer* newspaper. Although this is considered one of the more reputable British newspapers, it maintains a left-leaning bias and ultimately operates as a profit-making business through the sale of news. Although newspapers generally aim to ensure that they have evidence for the claims they make, much of this evidence comes from speaking directly to people involved or interested in the issue. That does not mean that the claims themselves are true as these sources may not be reliable or the quotations they provide may not be accurate reflections of what was meant or said.

5. Ask 'is there any additional evidence that strengthens or weakens the conclusion?'

There is additional, though circumspect, evidence that supports Alibhai-Brown's assertion that not enough is being done to promote diversity within LOCOG. The electronic link that points to LOCOG's Diversity and Inclusion team that Alibhai-Brown states was broken, was still not working several weeks after the article was published (this may or may not be due to embarrassment at the lack of diversity shown within it) and the only member of the team that I could find any information about was in an interesting blog post written by Diversity and Inclusion team member Ben Supple (Supple, 2009). In this post, Supple commended the fact that LOCOG wouldn't promote diversity under quota systems; which arguably lends support to Alibhai-Brown's view that LOCOG is, and will remain, heavily biased towards white men (which Supple openly categorises himself as).

6. Assess the plausibility of any explanation you have identified

One of the most plausible alternative explanations for the claim that the London Olympics is failing to live up to its promises on diversity is the findings of the EHRC report by Smallbone et al. (2008) of Kingston University, which concludes that the competing interests and restrictive legislation that the ODA operates under limits the actions that the Olympic Organising Committee can take. This indicates that any problems with ensuring diversity are not a demonstration of overt racist attitudes by those organising the games as implied by Alibhai-Brown.

7. Assess the appropriateness of any comparisons you have identified

There aren't any obvious comparisons that can be made although throughout her article, Alibhai-Brown suggests that this type of hypocrisy is typical of the British. Interestingly, she uses the term 'Perfidious Albion'; a negative term, particularly used by foreigners, to describe how Britain (England) is untrustworthy in its treatment and attitude towards non-natives. However the only real example that she provides is two unreferenced quotations by the former Conservative party leader Michael Howard, whereby in one he celebrates the diversity of London in his backing of the Olympic bid and in the other proposes limits on immigration. These are not, however, necessarily two mutually contradictory positions.

Ironically reader comments on Alibhai-Brown's article on the *Independent* website do support her prediction that she will be vilified for her criticism of British culture and the privilege that exists predominantly in support of white men from affluent backgrounds. Indeed, many of these comments, through racist language and attitudes, seem to unwittingly demonstrate support for some of the criticism that Alibhai-Brown is making.

8. Ask 'is there any reasoning that seems to be fallacious?'

There are several aspects of fallacious reasoning. The most notable one is the use of hearsay since many of the claims and sources provided by Alibhai-Brown originate from Doward's article rather than from more reliable sources.

The other large fallacious element in the article is the language and rhetoric used throughout. The tone is conversational and colloquial in nature and there are frequent emotive remarks and rhetorical questions. Most of which simply aim to add emphasis to her argument rather than provide real supporting evidence.

It could be suggested that Alibhai-Brown falls foul of the fallacy of appealing to authority when she uses Nelson Mandela in support for her critique. Although it could be accepted that Mandela is a figure who demonstrated support for inclusion in his transformation of South Africa (although this was predominantly the inclusion of one particular group), how he provides support for Alibhai-Brown's argument is unclear. That she cites him in both the title and conclusion suggests that she is using his name primarily to lend support to her argument.

9. Assess the logical structure of the argument

The basic structure of the argument is not made explicit but could be formulated as shown in Figure 7.3.

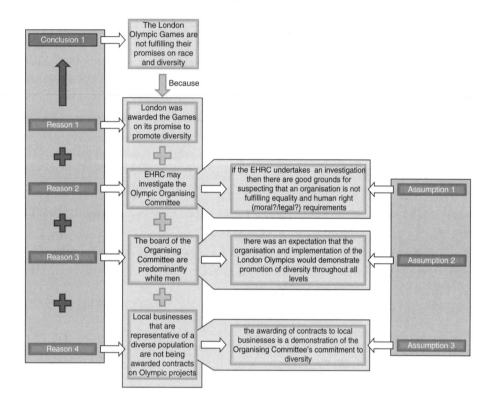

Figure 7.3.

10. Conclude, from your answers to points 1–9, whether overall it is a good argument

The fundamental claim made by Alibhai-Brown appears to be supported by reasonable evidence. However the reasons she provides are based on unstated and unsubstantiated assumptions, particularly the criticism she directs towards the members of the Organising Committee whom she states are 'unprincipled' and 'self-important'. In fact, evidence seems to suggest that the Organising Committee are making significant attempts to promote diversity in the organisation of the Games, with the use of their contractor website 'CompeteFor', and in the achievement of the Gold Standard. Evidence that demonstrates a lack of success in promoting diversity is arguably more due to conflicting interests, priorities and legislative requirements than a lack of value. However, the composition of the Organising Committee doesn't demonstrate diversity itself and this does seem to lend support to Alibhai-Brown's claim, especially as this is the very area where it has power to take action. That the EHRC may investigate LOCOG doesn't provide support to the argument either way since it isn't certain that the investigation will occur and the reasons and meaning attached to an investigation are unknown.

Alibhai-Brown's article needs to be taken for what it is, a comment piece in a national newspaper. Although some of the claims that are made have grounds for support, Alibhai-Brown herself provides no real evidence for them and instead she uses rhetoric as her primary tool for persuasion. Therefore, as an argument, it is not a particularly good one.

Learning Activity 7.1

Read the article in the following case study and using the assessment and evaluation diagrams (Figures 7.1 and 7.2), provide an analysis of the arguments made.

Case Study 7.2
The ascent of sport has reached its crisis point

We have lived through the ascent of sport. It is richer and grander than ever. In the 1980s newspapers devoted two pages to sport; now it is 20. Presidents genuflect at the feet of Olympic administrators, and football dominates the rhythm of the year like a religion.

Sport is dripping with glamour and influence. If, in 1950, you had bought a few shares in a company called 'professional sport ltd.', you would now be as rich as Warren Buffet. For players, administrators and pundits, sport is a massive gravy train that shows no sign of drying up.

It is tempting for everyone involved to keep the show on the road, to tow the party line, cash the cheques, and recycle the optimistic clichés.

The sporting bubble has never yet burst. But it will. I think it is starting to burst now. And soon we may have to decide which strands of sport we believe to be essential, and which superfluous – or worse than superfluous.

First, we need a little history. Professional sport was a giant accident. No one expected it. The Victorians glimpsed in amateur sport something astonishingly powerful. Sport could be a tool for building character and creating leaders. The Victorians had an Empire to run – and to civilize, as they saw it – and sport was their vehicle.

Yes, the Victorian moral hijacking of sport brought with it elements of snobbery and hypocrisy. But more importantly it gave sport a purpose. There is a reason why the Anglo-Saxon sports conquered the world: they were driven by an evangelical zeal.

This new moral dimension was sport's first giant stroke of luck. Sport transcended the narrow question of winning, and that became central to its democratic appeal. It was a form of education as much as entertainment.

So sport split off from mere entertainment: while an actress was seen as dangerously close to a prostitute, a sportsman was practically a prince. It is impossible to overstate the enduring influence of that legacy. The kudos of amateurism survived the transition into the age of professionalism. But for how much longer?

The second massive stroke of luck in the ascent of sport was television. It was television that made sportsmen rich, and now it oils the whole industry.

We have all been the beneficiaries of sport's two great accidents coming together: sport was highly respected when it became suddenly very rich. We have surfed that wave.

But professional sport's two accidental foundations – the moral dimension it inherited, and the financial riches it stumbled upon through television – have co-existed uneasily for 50 years. And now the marriage is falling apart. The unpleasant prospect looms: which parent do we want to live with? One is strict but inspirational, the other attractive but profligate.

The easy decision is to throw out the moral high ground, and say that sport is now just about entertainment and money. But I am unconvinced that the latter will flourish without the former. We will quickly tire of a never-ending athletic soap opera that lacks real heroes.

I am not saying that Thierry Henry's hand-ball will kill football. But a culture of non-stop cheating will eat away at sport's long-term appeal. One day a mother will look at the television screen, and say, 'Whatever happens, I will not let my son become a spitting, cheating professional sportsman.'

Parents make champions. And countless champions were first led onto the pitch by parents who hoped sport would be good for their kids, not because it offered a lucrative career. The talent base of sport owes far more to hope than it does to greed.

Nor will sport continue to draw upon patriotism. The ideal of representing your country above anything else is looking tragically out-of-date. Sport is now talked about as a never-ending series of shop windows. County cricket is the shop window for England, England is the shop window for the IPL, and the IPL – presumably – is the shop window for reality television.

These are not small shifts. They are seismic. The aftershocks will not be felt in 2012, or even 2020. But they may be irreversible. And sport will miss romance more than it thinks.

Sporting greatness lifts us most when it rubs shoulders with real life. The day after Roger Bannister broke the four-minute mile, he was held aloft by his fellow medical students. How much better to be among real friends in the pursuit of medicine than to 'celebrate' in an orchestrated open-top bus tour.

Sport has become used to believing the best is always yet to come. We have a nasty surprise ahead. Hubris is followed by nemesis.

'We look on past ages with condescension, as mere preparation for us,' wrote J.G. Farrell, 'but what if we're only an after-glow of them?'

[Smith, 2009]

Chapter Review

This chapter has attempted to put into practice some of the theory outlined in the preceding chapters. Its aim was to illustrate how an argument can be evaluated and assessed. However, there is only so much that a book of this type, and the learning activities it contains, can do to develop your critical thinking skills. Ultimately, it requires a questioning and sceptical, but honest and open, mind, a desire to learn and a commitment to continually practise. The development of such skills will arguably be worth it.

Further Reading

Fairbairn, GJ and Winch, C (1998) *Reading, Writing and Reasoning: A Guide for Students* (second edition). Buckingham: Open University Press. ★★★☆☆

Although it is not explicitly designed to be a book on critical thinking, it is included here as it deals with many of the aspects required for evaluating and constructing arguments. One of the most useful elements is its preliminary focus upon reading skills. Arguably, if you are unable to read and understand the arguments contained within the text you are focusing upon, then it is nigh on impossible to be able to effectively assess them. Therefore, this book provides useful tools in acquiring close reading skills as well as being able to formulate your own arguments through the written word.

Fisher, A (2004) *The Logic of Real Arguments* (second edition). Cambridge: Cambridge University Press. ★★★★☆

The Logic of Real Arguments is a comprehensive and detailed analysis of longer passages of argument. Each chapter deals with a specific argument from a range of sources and is underlined by the question, 'what evidence would be required to justify the acceptance of conclusion *X*?' Students of sport science-based courses might be most interested in the chapter on 'Evaluating "scientific" arguments'.

Metcalfe, M (2006) *Reading Critically at University*. London: Sage. ★★★☆☆

This book has a slightly different focus than other texts on critical thought in that it promotes the notion of a 'stance'. It is through viewing an argument from a particular 'stance' that we are able to offer a critique of it. As a result this book highlights the value of a pluralistic set of perspectives in order to develop the greatest range of understanding. One of the most helpful elements about this book is the way that it provides a thorough but clear analysis of passages of argument in order to show how such a critique is undertaken.

Thomson, A (2003) *Critical Reasoning: A Practical Introduction* (second edition). London: Routledge. ★★★★☆

Although I have mentioned this book in a previous chapter's further reading, it is worth mentioning again as its last chapter provides a really comprehensive overview of using reasoning skills when assessing longer passages of argument. It provides ten example exercises with detailed answers and so provides a good resource for students wanting to test their skills in this area.

Warburton, N (2006) *The Basics of Essay Writing*. Abingdon: Routledge. ★★★☆☆

Although this is a very useful general resource for students attempting to write good essays, Chapter 6 ('Making a Case') in particular covers the basics of creating an argument. It highlights the importance of 'signposting' to your audience what claim is being made and what reasons you are providing in support of it.

Answers to Learning Activities

Learning Activity 7.1

These are some general pointers and not a comprehensive evaluation of the arguments. I have tried, when possible, to give specific quotes from Smith's article to support my evaluation in order to demonstrate where the relevant information can be found.

1. Identify conclusion and reasons

The primary claim that Smith makes is that the sporting bubble is starting to burst and sport will not be able to sustain itself in the way it has done in the last 20 or so years. In other words, sport will inevitably enter a paradigm shift: 'Sport has become used to believing the best is always yet to come. We have a nasty surprise ahead. Hubris is followed by nemesis.'

(For clarification: 'hubris' means an arrogance resulting from excessive pride, whereas 'nemesis' means a just punishment. The phrase that Smith uses is equivalent to 'pride comes before a fall'.)

The reason he provides is:

- The two driving forces (the moral values we attach and the financial riches that make it viable as a business) that have created sport as we understand it today are fundamentally incompatible: 'But professional sport's two accidental foundations – the moral dimension it inherited, and the financial riches it stumbled upon through television – have co-existed uneasily for 50 years. And now the marriage is falling apart.'

This also acts as an intermediary conclusion that is (very weakly) supported by the following reasons:

- Sport is a wealth-creating asset by being a vehicle for mass entertainment and popular culture that people are prepared to pay for: 'Sport is dripping with glamour and influence. If, in 1950, you had bought a few shares in a company called 'professional sport ltd.', you would now be as rich as Warren Buffet. For players, administrators and pundits, sport is a massive gravy train that shows no sign of drying up' and 'Presidents genuflect at the feet of Olympic administrators, and football dominates the rhythm of the year like a religion.'
- The moral dimension believed to underpin sport allowed it to be used as an educational vehicle: 'Victorians glimpsed in amateur sport something astonishingly powerful. Sport could be a tool for building character and creating leaders.' For this reason, sports players and athletes were

respected and not seen merely as entertainers: 'while an actress was seen as dangerously close to a prostitute, a sportsman was practically a prince.'

Smith's argument could be seen to run as follows: the demands on professional athletes (by the private businesses that employ them) means that they are more likely to cheat as a means to their success (*this is implied not asserted*); the increase in cheating will mean that sport will no longer be seen as a means to provide moral education. Therefore parents will be less likely to encourage their children to participate in sport. Therefore the pool of talented athletes will be reduced and this in turn will reduce the quality of sport itself and therefore the entertainment value (*this is implied not asserted*). This will lead to a reduction in financial revenue, which will lead to the burst of the sporting bubble.

2. Identify unstated assumptions

The main assumption that is made is that sport as a business and sport as a means of moral education are contradictory. This can be expressed as an either/or argument:

Either sport is a business or it is a means of moral education. (*P* or *Q*.)

3. Evaluating the truth of reasons/assumptions

Smith takes the former unstated assumption as self-evident although he does state that sport has developed 'a culture of non-stop cheating' and cites Henry's handball in the France/Ireland 2009 World Cup qualifier as an example of this. The implicit assumption here is that this culture has developed due to the commodification of sport. However, to assess whether there really is more cheating in sport today than before the advent of professionalism and commercialism requires evidence. There may be an argument that as players and athletes are employed to bring success (and the revenue and profits that come from this success) to their team then there is a greater demand on them to succeed (at whatever cost, which may included cheating) since their livelihood is at stake, but an argument along these lines would require further development.

Smith supports his view that an essential element of sport (and one that makes sport valuable) is its moral purpose by providing reference to the Victorians who saw it as a way to build and civilise empires. Although there is reasonable and reliable evidence to suggest that sport was promoted as a way of instilling particular moral values (discipline, adherence to rules, leadership, etc.) it is less accepted that this was the only conception of sport. Even if we accept Smith's view of sport it still requires a leap of faith to accepting that this therefore means that cheating was less prevalent then than it is now. It may be proposed that Smith views this supposed golden age of moral sport through rose- (or gold-) tinted glasses.

Smith's reference to Henry's handball incident may weaken his argument as there is no evidence to suggest that it was an act of cheating, if we take cheating to mean a deliberate intention to break the rules and deceive others. Arguably, Henry did not intend to break the rule and deceive the officials and was embarrassed and contrite when a goal was the outcome. Admittedly there is a much greater discussion to have on this topic of cheating, but perhaps the example of Henry does not support Smith's claim that sport has developed into a 'non-stop culture of cheating'.

Furthermore, it contradicts Smith's claim that sport no longer is able 'to draw upon patriotism' as Henry's action not to tell the officials of the infringement at the time may have been driven by the knowledge that he would have been vilified by his own countrymen had he have done so.

On this point, Smith maintains that the money associated with professional sport means that representing one's country is considered less valuable than representing a particular private club or team. Smith cites the development of the Indian Premier League (IPL) to support his view. There is evidence to suggest that there has been a conflict of interest between the demands of international test match cricket and the privately run IPL. There is similar evidence of such conflict in other professional sports, notably rugby and football. However, whether the riches offered by private leagues inevitably signals the demise of international representation needs further assessment.

4. Assess the reliability of any authorities on whom the reasoning depends

Smith's article is an opinion piece and attempts to use logical reasoning to persuade his audience. Therefore it does not rely on any specific authority or evidence. The only authority quoted is that of J.G. Farrell and a line from his fictional story *The Siege of Krishnapur* on the British occupation of India. Through this quote, Smith is drawing a comparison between the uprising of the indigenous population at a time of perceived tranquillity, and modern sport.

5. Ask 'is there any additional evidence that strengthens or weakens the conclusion?'

There may be good evidence that shows that sports men and women do not see their (moral) roles and responsibility any differently in the professional era than they did in the amateur era but this would require some deeper research.

As stated in my evaluation of Smith's reference to Henry's handball, there is a case that it provides evidence against Smith's claims regarding a culture of cheating and a lack of patriotism.

There is also perhaps a case to be made regarding the implementation of technology that ensures that a culture of 'non-stop cheating' is less likely today than in previous decades. Though this may lead to players abdicating any moral responsibility to ensure they play fairly out of duty rather than consequence, it may ultimately refute Smith's predictions of parents no longer wishing their children to play sport. Smith's prediction is based upon parents' seeing a negative view of sport (one that involves 'non-stop cheating') but if technology is in place that means players don't cheat (because they know they will not get away with it) then this view of sport will not be demonstrated. The assumption here is that children see sports players and athletes as role models and replicate their behaviour.

6. Assess the plausibility of any explanation you have identified

As stated in the previous point, the implementation of technology at the top of the game may mean that Smith's predictions for sport do not manifest themselves. Businesses involved in making money through sport cannot guarantee their success through any means since they still have to abide by the rules set down by the sport's governing body (Speedo's 'shark-skin' swim suit is a case in point). Although Smith fears that the commercialisation of sport will lead to it becoming more about entertainment than a demonstration of the capabilities of the human spirit (sport being represented by things such as WWE wrestling rather than Roger Bannister moments) as Smith himself states, it is unlikely that the general public will be satisfied with this conception of sport: 'we will quickly tire of a never-ending athletic soap opera that lacks real heroes'.

7. Assess the appropriateness of any comparisons you have identified

As shown by his last remarks, Smith draws comparison between previous episodes in history when arrogance has led to a downfall and modern sport. Further evaluation is needed to assess whether those involved in modern sport can really be said to be 'arrogant' and whether it is inevitable that there will be a subsequent downfall.

8. Ask 'is there any reasoning that seems to be fallacious?'

Although Smith writes eloquently and persuasively, he does have a tendency for over-exaggeration. Additionally, much of his persuasive rhetoric is an appeal to emotion. He frequently uses the term 'we' in an attempt to display fraternity with his audience. He also appeals to history by giving a fairly rose-tinted view of sport before the age of professionalism. For instance, his use of the Bannister example is an attempt to persuade his audience of a bygone age of which we fondly reminisce.

9. Assess the logical structure of the argument

There appears to be some logical structure to Smith's main argument but its validity depends on the assumption that commercial business and the values of sport are incompatible. As discussed in point three, Smith's use of the Henry example might prove contradictory to the claim that he makes.

10. Conclude, from your answers to points 1–9, whether overall it is a good argument

Smith appears to make a fairly persuasive argument but most of this seems to be due to his appeal to our emotions. He doesn't provide any good evidence to support his claims and therefore there is no real reason to believe his conclusion to be true.

References

Alibhai-Brown, Y (2009) The London Olympics are failing their racial promises: time to make sure the games are what Mandela believed they could be. The *Independent*. Monday 21 December. www.independent.co.uk/opinion/commentators/yasmin-alibhai-brown/yasmin-alibhaibrown-the-london-olympics-are-failing-their-racial-promises-1846450.html. Accessed December 2009.

Archery Factsheet (2008) *Active People Survey 2 2007/08*. Sport England publication. www.sportengland.org/research/active_people_survey/active_people_survey2.aspx. Accessed February 2010.

Beaumont, C (2009) London 2012 blog. www.london2012.com/blog/2009/12/gareth-thomas-coming-out-and-why-it-s-important-for-spor.php. Accessed January 2010.

Blackburn, S (2001) *Think: A Compelling Introduction to Philosophy*. Oxford: Oxford University Press.

Bonnett, A (2001) *How to Argue: A Students' Guide*. Harlow: Pearson Education Limited.

Bowell, T and Kemp, G (2005) *Critical Thinking: A Concise Guide* (second edition). London: Routledge.

Bradshaw, B (2009) www.equalityhumanrights.com/uploaded_files/PSD/kinghamresponse.docx. Accessed January 2010.

Brown, A and Beyerstein, D (2003) *Critical Thinking: The Three Rs of College Life: Reading, Reasoning and wRiting*. Department of Philosophy: Langara College. www.langara.bc.ca/liberal-arts/philosophy/media/PDFs/criticalthinking.pdf. Accessed January 2010.

CompeteFor. www.competefor.com/business/visionAndObjectives.html;jsessionid=B891C74 BB9F0380A427221D9862DC681.server1. Accessed January 2010.

Cottrell, S (2005) *Critical Thinking Skills: Developing Effective Analysis and Argument*. Basingstoke: Palgrave Macmillan.

Critical Thinking Web. Hong Kong University. www.philosophy.hku.hk/think/. Accessed January 2010.

Crow, G (2005) *The Art of Sociological Argument*. Basingstoke: Palgrave Macmillan.

Cryan, D, Shatil, S and Mayblin, B (2008) *Introducing Logic: A Graphic Guide*. Royston: Icon Books.

DebateWise. www.debatewise.org/categories/sport. Accessed January 2010.

Department of Culture, Media and Sport Annual Report (2008) www.culture.gov.uk/images/publications/DCMS_Annual_Report_08_01.pdf. Accessed October 2009.

Doward, J (2009) Sebastian Coe's London Olympics team in row with equality watchdog. The *Observer*. Sunday 20 December. www.guardian.co.uk/uk/2009/dec/20/coe-olympics-equality-row. Accessed January 2010.

Eastwood, M (2003) *Principles of Human Nutrition* (second edition). Oxford: Blackwell.

Ennis, R (1996) *Critical Thinking*. London: Prentice-Hall.

Facey, D (2009) Wiley can sue 'bully' Fergie. The *Sun*, 12 October.

Facione, P (2007) Critical thinking: what it is and why it counts. Insight Assessment: California Academic Press. www.insightassessment.com/pdf_files/what&why2006.pdf. Accessed January 2010.

Fairbairn, GJ and Winch, C (1998) *Reading, Writing and Reasoning: A Guide for Students* (second edition). Buckingham: Open University Press.

Fisher, A (2001) *Critical Thinking: An Introduction*. Cambridge: Cambridge University Press.

Fisher, A (2004) *The Logic of Real Arguments* (second edition). Cambridge: Cambridge University Press.

Garnham, A and Oakhill, J (1994) *Thinking and Reasoning*. Oxford: Blackwell.

Hacking, I (2001) *An Introduction to Probability and Inductive Logic*. Cambridge: Cambridge University Press.

Hamblin, CL (1970) *Fallacies*. London: Methuen.

Hare, W (2001) Bertrand Russell on critical thinking. *Journal of Thought*, 36, 1: 7–16. www.criticalthinking.org/articles/bertrand-russell.cfm. Accessed January 2010.

Harman, N (2009) Richard Gasquet cleared of doping after innocent kiss. The *Times*. 17 December 2009. www.timesonline.co.uk/tol/sport/tennis/article6960667.ece. Accessed December 2009.

Hislop, L (2008) The *Times*. 28 May.

Hume, PA and Paton, CD (2008) Sports nutrition and more at the 2008 AAESS Conference. *Sports Science* 12: 25–30. www.sportsci.org/2008/pahcdp.htm. Accessed February 2010.

Johnson-Laird, P (2006) *How We Reason*. Oxford: Oxford University Press.

Kuhn, T (1977) *The Essential Tension. Selected Studies in Scientific Tradition and Change*. Chicago: University of Chicago Press, pp321–22.

Lau, J and Chan, J *Critical Thinking Community: The Foundation for Critical Thinking*. www.criticalthinking.org/. Accessed January 2010.

London Development Agency (2009) London Development Agency Awards LOCOG Gold for Diversity. Press release. 18 December. www.lda.gov.uk/server.php?show=ConWebDoc.3530. Accessed January 2010.

Metcalfe, M (2006) *Reading Critically at University*. London: Sage.

Moon, J (2008) *Critical Thinking: An Exploration of Theory and Practice*. London: Routledge.

Nosich, GM (2009) *Learning to Think Things Through: A Guide to Critical Thinking Across the Curriculum* (third edition). Upper Saddle River, NJ: Pearson Prentice-Hall.

Passmore, J (1967) On teaching to be critical, in Peters, RS (ed) *The Concept of Education*. London: Routledge & Kegan Paul, pp192–211.

Paul, R and Elder, L (2002) *Critical Thinking: Tools for Taking Charge of Your Professional and Personal Life*. Upper Saddle River, NJ: FT Press.

Paul, R and Elder, L (2004a) *The Miniature Guide to Critical Thinking: Concepts and Tools* (fourth edition). Dillon Beach, CA: The Foundation for Critical Thinking.

Paul, R and Elder, L (2004b) *The Thinker's Guide to Fallacies: The Art of Mental Trickery and Manipulation* (fourth edition). Dillon Beach, CA: The Foundation for Critical Thinking.

Phelen, P and Reynolds, P (1996) *Argument and Evidence: A Critical Analysis for the Social Sciences.* London: Routledge.

Phillips, T (2005) Let's show the world its future. The *Observer.* Sunday 20 July. www.guardian.co.uk/uk/2005/jul/10/olympics2012.olympicgames. Accessed February 2010.

Pirie, M (2006) *How to Win Every Argument: The Use and Abuse of Logic.* London: Continuum.

Porter, BF (2002) *The Voice of Reason: Fundamentals of Critical Thinking.* Oxford: Oxford University Press.

Powers, SK and Howley, ET (2007) *Exercise Physiology and Application to Fitness and Performance* (sixth edition). London: McGraw-Hill.

ProCon.org. www.procon.org/. Accessed January 2010.

Radford, B (2008) Ascot acts to prevent 'meat' trade at sales. The *Guardian.* 26 November 2008.

Reid, HL (2009) Has the science of sport outpaced philosophy of sport? *Philosophy of Sport Blog.* www.philosophyandsports.blogspot.com/2009/09/has-science-of-sport-outpaced.html. Accessed October 2009.

Reid, SP (2002) *How to Think: Building Your Mental Muscle.* London: Prentice-Hall.

Ronay, B (2009) BBC's British bias spoils swimming's polyurethane pantomime. The *Guardian.* 3 August 2009. www.guardian.co.uk/sport/blog/2009/aug/03/fina-world-swimming-championships-tv. Accessed August 2009.

Scriven, M (1976) *Reasoning.* London: McGraw-Hill.

Smallbone, D, Kitching, J, Athayde, R and Xheneti, M (2008) Procurement and supplier diversity in the 2012 Olympics. EHRC Research Report 6. Kingston University. www.equalityhuman rights.com/uploaded_files/research/procurement_in_2012_olympics.pdf. Accessed December 2009.

Smith, E (2009) The ascent of sport has reached its crisis point. The *Telegraph.* 27 November 2009. www.telegraph.co.uk/sport/6672488/The-ascent-of-sport-has-reached-its-crisis-point.html. Accessed January 2010.

Sports Life (2009) The *Telegraph.* www.telegraph.co.uk/sponsored/sport/sportslife/6416543/Athletics-what-makes-Usain-Bolt-the-fastest-man-on-the-planet.html. Accessed December 2009.

Supple, B (2009) London 2010 blog. www.london2012.com/blog/2009/08/will-london-2012-diversity-and-inclusion-targets-create-.php. Accessed January 2010.

Taleb, N (2008) *The Black Swan.* London: Penguin.

Thomson, A (1999) *Critical Reasoning in Ethics: A Practical Introduction.* London: Routledge.

Thomson, A [1996] (2003) *Critical Reasoning: A Practical Introduction* (second edition). London: Routledge.

Tindale, C (2007) *Fallacies and Argument Appraisal.* Cambridge: Cambridge University Press.

Uth, N (2005) Anthropometric comparison of world-class sprinters and normal populations. *Journal of Sport Science and Medicine,* 4: 608–16.

Van den Brink-Budgen, R (2000) *Critical Thinking for Students* (third edition). Oxford: Howtobooks.

Warburton, N (2000) *Thinking from A to Z* (second edition). London: Routledge.

Warburton, N (2006) *The Basics of Essay Writing*. Abingdon: Routledge.

Weston, A (2000) *A Rulebook for Arguments* (third edition). Cambridge: Hackett Publishing Company.

Whannel, G (2008) *Culture, Politics and Sport: Blowing the Whistle Revisited*. Abingdon: Routledge.

Index